4/03

The 1993 World Trade Center Bombing

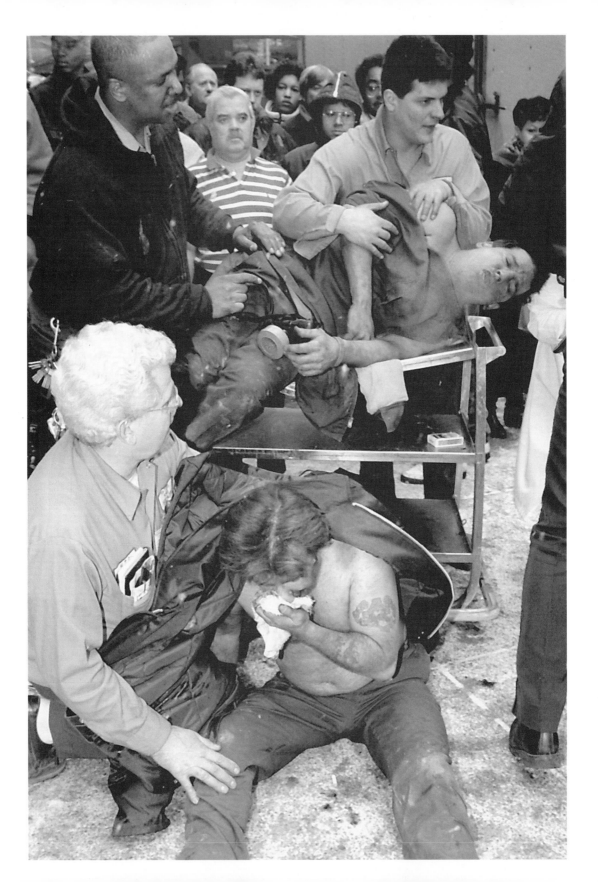

The 1993 World Trade Center Bombing

Charles J. Shields

CHELSEA HOUSE PUBLISHERS

Philadelphia

Frontispiece: Victims of the bomb explosion at the World Trade Center are treated at the scene. The catastrophe, which took the lives of six people, made Americans question how safe they are against terrorist attacks.

CHELSEA HOUSE PUBLISHERS

Editor in Chief Sally Cheney
Director of Production Kim Shinners
Production Manager Pamela Loos
Art Director Sara Davis
Production Editor Diann Grasse

Staff for THE WORLD TRADE CENTER BOMBING

Senior Editor LeeAnne Gelletly
Assistant Editor Brian Baughan
Cover Designer Takeshi Takahashi
Layout by 21st Century Publishing and Communications, Inc.

First Printing

1 3 5 7 9 8 6 4 2

The Chelsea House World Wide Web address is
http://www.chelseahouse.com

Library of Congress Cataloging-in-Publication Data

Shields, Charles J., 1951–
    The World Trade Center bombing / Charles J. Shields
        p. cm. — (Great disasters, reforms and ramifications)
    Includes bibliographical references and index.
    ISBN 0-7910-5789-5 (alk. paper)
        1. World Trade Center Bombing, New York, N.Y., 1993
    —Juvenile literature. 2. Terrorism—New York (State)—
    New York. 3. Bombings—New York (State)—New York.
    [1. World Trade Center Bombing, New York, N.Y., 1993.
    2. Terrorism. 3. Bombings.] I. Title II. Series.

HV6432.S544 2001
364.1'09747'1—dc21
                                                    2001028794

Contents

GREAT DISASTERS
REFORMS and RAMIFICATIONS

Jill McCaffrey
National Chairman
Armed Forces Emergency Services
American Red Cross

Introduction

Disasters have always been a source of fascination and awe. Tales of a great flood that nearly wipes out all life are among humanity's oldest recorded stories, dating at least from the second millennium B.C., and they appear in cultures from the Middle East to the Arctic Circle to the southernmost tip of South America and the islands of Polynesia. Typically gods are at the center of these ancient disaster tales—which is perhaps not too surprising, given the fact that the tales originated during a time when human beings were at the mercy of natural forces they did not understand.

To a great extent, we still are at the mercy of nature, as anyone who reads the newspapers or watches nightly news broadcasts can attest.

Hurricanes, earthquakes, tornados, wildfires, and floods continue to exact a heavy toll in suffering and death, despite our considerable knowledge of the workings of the physical world. If science has offered only limited protection from the consequences of natural disasters, it has in no way diminished our fascination with them. Perhaps that's because the scale and power of natural disasters force us as individuals to confront our relatively insignificant place in the physical world and remind us of the fragility and transience of our lives. Perhaps it's because we can imagine ourselves in the midst of dire circumstances and wonder how we would respond. Perhaps it's because disasters seem to bring out the best and worst instincts of humanity: altruism and selfishness, courage and cowardice, generosity and greed.

As one of the national chairmen of the American Red Cross, a humanitarian organization that provides relief for victims of disasters, I have had the privilege of seeing some of humanity's best instincts. I have witnessed communities pulling together in the face of trauma; I have seen thousands of people answer the call to help total strangers in their time of need.

Of course, helping victims after a tragedy is not the only way, or even the best way, to deal with disaster. In many cases planning and preparation can minimize damage and loss of life—or even avoid a disaster entirely. For, as history repeatedly shows, many disasters are caused not by nature but by human folly, shortsightedness, and unethical conduct. For example, when a land developer wanted to create a lake for his exclusive resort club in Pennsylvania's Allegheny Mountains in 1880, he ignored expert warnings and cut corners in reconstructing an earthen dam. On May 31, 1889, the dam gave way, unleashing 20 million tons of water on the towns below. The Johnstown Flood, the deadliest in American history, claimed more than 2,200 lives. Greed and negligence would figure prominently in the Triangle Shirtwaist Company fire in 1911. Deplorable conditions in the garment sweatshop, along with a failure to give any thought to the safety of workers, led to the tragic deaths of 146 persons. Technology outstripped wisdom only a year later, when the designers of the luxury liner *Titanic* smugly declared their state-of-the-art ship "unsinkable," seeing no need to provide lifeboat capacity for everyone onboard. On the night of April 14, 1912, more than 1,500 passengers and crew paid for this hubris with their lives after the ship collided with an iceberg and sank. But human catastrophes aren't always the unforeseen consequences of carelessness or folly. In the 1940s the leaders of Nazi Germany purposefully and systematically set out to exterminate all Jews, along with Gypsies, homosexuals, the mentally ill, and other so-called undesirables. More recently terrorists have targeted random members of society, blowing up airplanes and buildings in an effort to advance their political agendas.

The books in the GREAT DISASTERS: REFORMS AND RAMIFICATIONS series examine these and other famous disasters, natural and human made. They explain the causes of the disasters, describe in detail how events unfolded, and paint vivid portraits of the people caught up in dangerous circumstances. But these books are more than just accounts of what happened to whom and why. For they place the disasters in historical perspective, showing how people's attitudes and actions changed and detailing the steps society took in the wake of each calamity. And in the end, the most important lesson we can learn from any disaster—as well as the most fitting tribute to those who suffered and died—is how to avoid a repeat in the future.

The World Trade Center,
located in the heart of
the financial district of
New York City, stands
110 stories high. Terrorists
targeted the landmark
building in hopes of killing
as many as 225,000
people in the towers and
on the streets below.

A Trail of Blood

In February 1993, a group of terrorists in Brooklyn, New York, assembled a 1,500-pound bomb. Their target—the World Trade Center in downtown New York City. To them and their conspirators, the building served as the ideal American landmark for the worst act of domestic terrorism in United States history.

The twin towers of the World Trade Center rise one-third of a mile over lower Manhattan. From the open-air observation deck on the 110th floor of the second tower (dubbed WTC 2), visitors are treated to a panoramic view of the city—when weather is good one can see as far as 55 miles away. Far below, on the Brooklyn and Manhattan Bridges, cars and trucks that seem impossibly small appear to glide back and forth. Included in the admission price to the outside deck is a six-minute simulated helicopter ride through the city over the Verrazano Bridge, through Central Park, and into Times Square.

At the visitors' center, tourists can also view an exhibit called "Everything You Ever Wondered About the World Trade Center and More." Designed by architects Minoru Yamasaki and Emery Roth, the World Trade Center was completed in 1973. Spanning 16 acres, the seven-building complex contains restaurants, a 60-store shopping mall, and the world-class Vista hotel. The World Trade Center lobby is decorated with original works by contemporary artists, and musical performances are staged throughout the year.

When most people in New York City think of the World Trade Center, however, they think only of its soaring twin towers. Constructed using 200,000 tons of steel, 425,000 cubic yards of concrete, and 43,600 windows, the towers are so enormous that they have separate postal zip codes. Every floor contains an acre of office space—12 million square feet in all, or 10 percent of all available office space in Manhattan's busy financial district. The number of people inside the World Trade Center on an average weekday is about 55,000—exceeding the population of many American towns.

On a typical workday at noon, the financial district is one of the most densely populated places on earth. That fact was one of the reasons why, on September 16, 1920, a bomber planted a device in a horse-drawn wagon near the Morgan Guaranty Trust Co., just a few blocks from the present World Trade Center. The bomb exploded at midday, killing 40 people and injuring 200. The walls of the Morgan Guaranty building still bear the blast marks of the explosion. Police were never able to solve the crime. More than 70 years later, in 1993, the terrorists who sized up the World Trade Center wanted far more destruction and loss of life. If all went well, they imagined, their

explosives would send one of the mighty towers crashing into its twin, causing a cataclysmic disaster that would kill one-quarter of a million people.

A panoramic view of New York City as seen from the World Trade Center outdoor observation deck.

Like a trail of blood, the devastation that occurred at the World Trade Center could be traced back three years earlier with the murder of Meir Kahane. During the 1950s, Martin David Kahane had changed his name when he became a rabbi (religious teacher) for a congregation of Orthodox Jews in New York City's Queens borough. In 1960, despite his affiliation with the strongly traditional Orthodox branch of Judaism, Kahane founded the Jewish Defense League (JDL). Its initial purpose was to sponsor safety patrols and to

Terrorists had targeted New York City's financial district, the heart of the nation's economy, as early as September 16, 1920, when a bomb was placed in a wagon outside the Morgan Guaranty Trust Company. The resulting explosion killed 40 people and injured 200.

serve as a response network against acts of anti-Semitism, but the group was radical. Rabbinical students in the JDL, for example, received training in self-defense and in paramilitary tactics. Many proudly repeated the slogan "Every Jew a .22"—meaning that every Jew should be armed with a rifle for his own defense.

Gradually, Kahane shifted his attention to world matters and began an outspoken campaign about the treatment of Jews in the Soviet Union. In 1971, he emigrated to Israel; 13 years later he was elected to the Knesset (the Israeli parliament). He led the Kach Party, which was known for inflammatory anti-Palestinian and anti-Arab politics. Kahane called for the complete removal of Arabs from Israel and all its territories. His critics labeled his tactics undemocratic and Nazi-like, and in 1988 the Israeli government banned the Kach Party from elections. Nevertheless, the party continued to receive strong support from many Israelis and Jewish Americans.

On November 5, 1990, Kahane delivered a speech to 70 people in the conference room of a New York City hotel. Just as he finished, a man stepped forward, aimed a .357-caliber revolver at Kahane, and shot and killed him at point-blank range. As the gunman fled, he also shot an elderly bystander. Outside, he ordered a cab driver at gunpoint to drive him down the block, then jumped out to continue his escape on foot. A U.S. Postal Service policeman named Carlos Acosta ordered the gunman to stop. The gunman fired, striking Acosta in his bulletproof vest. Although wounded, Acosta returned fire and finally stopped the fleeing man with a shot to the neck.

The assailant was El Sayyid Nosair, an Egyptian national and a Muslim. He lived in New Jersey with his American wife and child and worked as an electrician for New York State. As Nosair recovered from his wound in a hospital, 15,000 mourners attended Kahane's funeral in Israel. A year later, in November 1991, Nosair stood trial for the murder of Meir Kahane.

Nosair's trial became a rallying point among local Muslim fundamentalists, who turned out in force to support the man they believed was a hero. Attorney William Kunstler, who had achieved fame for taking on high-profile, controversial cases, served as the assailant's lawyer. Kunstler made no secret of his own dislike of Kahane. He would later say in an interview, "I guess I felt that maybe [Nosair had] done a good thing in getting rid of Meir Kahane." During the trials, emotions ran high, with Kunstler receiving death threats and unspent bullets in the mail. Angry supporters of Kahane carved "Death to Kunstler" and "Death to Nosair" on the walls of elevators in the downtown New York City courthouse where the trial took place.

Kunstler's strategy was simple: he argued that his

client was not guilty "beyond a reasonable doubt," which is the standard by which those accused of a crime are judged in American courts. He pummeled the jury with a flurry of questions: What did the videotape of the murder scene really show? Why did the autopsy of Kahane's body fail to establish where the bullet had come from? Could eyewitnesses, most of whom were Kahane supporters, be trusted? At one point during the trial, Kunstler said, Kahane's son assaulted him in the courtroom, and once during a press conference, the son had to be subdued at gunpoint by the lawyer's armed bodyguards.

Although the jury found Nosair guilty on a weapons violation, it reached a verdict of not guilty on the charge of murder. Outside the courtroom after the trial concluded, Nosair's jubilant supporters cheered and congratulated the lawyer. A tall, husky, red-haired man named Mahmud Abouhalima hoisted Kunstler onto his shoulders and carried him above the crowd. The trial judge sentenced Nosair to seven years in Attica Correctional Facility in upstate New York.

During the investigation of the murder, detectives had searched Nosair's home for evidence and discovered notes in his handwriting about attacks on the "enemies of Islam." These attacks, the notes read, would be carried out by "destroying the structure of their civilized pillars such as the touristic infrastructure . . . and their high world buildings which they are proud of and their statues . . . and the buildings in which their leaders gather."

Such alarming language was commonly heard at the Alkifah Refugee Center on Atlantic Avenue in Brooklyn, where Nosair, Mahmud Abouhalima, and other Muslims gathered. The center was run by a fiery Islamic scholar named Sheik Omar Abdel-Rahman. Blind, obese, and diabetic, the 56-year-old sheik dressed in flowing white robes. He exerted a mesmerizing force not only over the

Defense attorney William Kunstler waves his hat in celebration, acknowledging his victory in the acquittal of El Sayyid Nosair on the charge of murdering Rabbi Kahane. Nosair was sentenced to jail for seven years for a weapons violation.

members of the center but also over those who gathered for formal prayer at the Al-Salam Mosque, a converted third-floor warehouse in Jersey City, not far from the refugee center. "He is like my father," one of his followers told a *Newsweek* reporter. In private, many of his disciples kissed his hand as a gesture of reverence.

The refugee center was commonly called the "*jihad* office" by residents of the Brooklyn neighborhood where it was located. In Islam, the dominant religion of many portions of North Africa, the Middle East, and the Near East, *jihad* usually translates to mean a "holy war" waged against enemies of the faith. To more modern Muslim scholars, the term also refers to a spiritual and moral "striving in the path of God." As they listened to Abdel-Rahman preach, young Muslim men trying to make their way in a strange country far from their homelands heard a call to wage a righteous battle for Islam and for Allah (God) himself.

"The laws of God have been usurped by [Christian] Crusaders' laws," Abdel-Rahman wrote in his 1985 autobiography. "The hand of a thief is not cut off, the drinker of liquor is not whipped, the adulterer is not stoned [as he should be]. Islamic holy law should be followed to the letter." During one sermon, he urged his followers to "hit hard and kill the enemies of God in every spot," and he assured one congregation that "assassination for the sake of rendering Islam triumphant is legitimate." During an interview with a follower, Abdel-Rahman once said, "We have to be terrorists. . . . The Great Allah said, 'Against them make ready your strength to the utmost of your power, including steeds of war, to strike terror into the enemies of Allah.'"

The sheik founded his beliefs on the teachings of the 14th-century Muslim philosopher Ibn Taimiyya. Taimiyya argued that devout Muslims had a duty to assassinate any Muslim leader who did not abide by *shariah,* the law of Islam. An attorney who represented Abdel-Rahman in Egypt in legal battles with the state said of the sheik, "He is a man who holds to his opinions when he feels that they are the right opinions, and he is not afraid of the government or any other authority."

Abdel-Rahman was born in 1938 in the village of Al Gamalia in Egypt. He went blind when he was less than a year old, probably from water-borne parasites or disease. As was the custom, relatives took him to a mosque in the hope he might learn to preach. By age 11 he had memorized the entire Koran (the Islamic holy book), an achievement that earned him admission to boarding school. From there he attended Al Azar University in Cairo, considered the height of Islamic education. After he graduated in 1965, his superiors assigned him to a small mosque on the outskirts of the town of Fayoum, 60 miles south of Cairo.

Abdel-Rahman's first brush with Egyptian authorities came in September 1970, with the death of Egypt's worldly president, Gamal Abdel Nasser. Millions of Egyptians mourned Nasser—but not Abdel-Rahman. He had blasted the president in his sermons as "the wicked Pharoah." Abdel-Rahman later wrote, "The state allows adultery and creates the opportunity for it. The state organizes nightclubs and prepares special police to protect adulterers and prostitutes. Liquor factories are built by the state. Doesn't this deny God's laws?" he railed. At the time of Nasser's death, the sheik told his followers not to pray for the leader's soul because he had been an infidel (a nonbeliever). To prevent political unrest stemming from Abdel-Rahman's rhetoric, Egyptian officials detained him without charges for eight months in Cairo's ancient Citadel Prison.

After his release, Abdel-Rahman taught briefly at a girls' school in Asyut, then journeyed to Saudi Arabia. There, according to some sources, he came in contact with leaders of a movement that called for a return to militant Islam—a campaign that advocated spreading the religion by force. The influence of that movement had been seen during a routine military parade in Cairo in 1981 during which Egyptian president Anwar Sadat was assassinated. Sadat had been making gradual but important progress in finding a peaceful solution to his country's stormy relationship with Israel. That day, a vehicle passing the viewing stand where the president and other dignitaries stood unexpectedly swung out of formation and approached the stand. Assassins in the vehicle sprayed a barrage of automatic weapon and machine-gun fire into the seats, killing Sadat and several others.

The Egyptian government indicted 24 conspirators in the attack, all members of the extremist Islamic Group in the Egyptian military. Four of them were executed.

Supporters of the accused rioted in Asyut, killing 100 policeman, and in the fallout police also arrested Abdel-Rahman. They claimed that his rabble-rousing sermons had encouraged both the presidential assassination and the ensuing riots.

On trial, however, Abdel-Rahman made an intimidating witness as he championed the sanctity of Islamic law. At times, his prosecutors were left fumbling and speechless. He was acquitted, and successfully sued the Egyptian government for allegedly torturing him while he was imprisoned. Abdel-Rahman's influence and leadership, not only in his faith but also in the ferocious arena of Arab politics, earned him the honorary title of sheik. It also earned him many powerful rivals.

In the 1980s the dusty town of Peshawar, Pakistan, became the staging ground for Islamic freedom fighters. They traveled through the nearby Khyber Pass to fight in the deeply Islamic country of Afghanistan, which was occupied by Soviet troops. Abdel-Rahman journeyed to Peshawar twice to inspire the 10,000 Arab-Afghans headed for their homeland. While there, he stayed at the home of Mohammed Islamouli, the brother of the man who had organized Anwar Sadat's assassination.

The call to fight the Soviets in Afghanistan had been issued by Abdullah Azzam, a Palestinian scholar, former professor of Islamic Law, and idolized teacher at Jordan University. One of his students was Mohammed Salameh. Azzam's support of the guerilla war in Afghanistan inspired deep loyalty in young Arabs like Salameh, especially those who lived in the disputed territory of Palestine. For Azzam and his followers, the battle against the Soviet Union was a *jihad*.

To broaden the movement, Azzam sent a trusted lieutenant, Mustafa Shalabi, to the United States. There, Shalabi quickly attracted a following at storefront

Minutes before his assassination by Muslim extremists, Egyptian president Anwar Sadat salutes officers during a review of the military. Up until his death in 1981, Sadat had worked to improve Egypt's relations with its neighbor Israel.

mosques in Brooklyn, New York, and Jersey City, New Jersey. He traveled to other American cities and even to Canada, delivering ardent speeches that called for Islam to prevail over its enemies. He chose as his North American headquarters the refugee center on Atlantic

Omar Abdel-Rahman, jailed in Cairo on charges of assassinating the Egyptian president Anwar Sadat, insisted he was innocent at his trial. His bold testimony earned him a reputation among both his enemies and his followers, who thereafter honored him with the title of sheik.

Avenue—the *jihad* office. He also offered weapons training at a Connecticut shooting range.

One of Shalabi's pupils in 1989 was El Sayyid Nosair, who shot Meir Kahane the following year. Shalabi selected as his assistant Mahmud Abouhalima, the Egyptian cab driver and war veteran who would carry attorney William Kunstler on his shoulders after Nosair's acquittal.

At the time Shalabi established himself in the United States, the Egyptian government was cracking down on the spread of Islamic fundamentalism. Chief among its targets was Sheik Omar Abdel-Rahman, accused by the government of issuing *fatwas*—orders to the faithful— to kill Christians. The sheik denied the charges; to his followers, however, Abdel-Rahman told a different tale.

He described his absolute right to issue *fatwas* against enemies like Anwar Sadat and Meir Kahane as an "honor and something to be proud of. We ask God to make us worthy of it, that we be worthy to issue a *fatwa* to kill tyrants, oppressors, and infidels."

Despite being placed under house arrest and guarded by Egyptian soldiers, the blind cleric escaped with the help of his followers. One of his disciples claimed that the sheik was carried out of the house hidden inside a washing machine. Another claimed that an impostor dressed to look like Abdel-Rahman distracted the guards while the cleric was spirited away. In any case, in 1990 Abdel-Rahman showed up at the U.S. embassy in Sudan and requested a visa to visit the United States. Although he was listed on a U.S. State Department "watch list" as someone not permitted to enter the country, a computer foul-up allowed him to obtain the visa. After a short trip to Pakistan, Abdel-Rahman entered the United States.

Almost immediately after Abdel-Rahman's arrival in New York, trouble erupted at the Brooklyn refugee center. He and Shalabi quarreled over the center's main purpose. The sheik interpreted the Koran, for example, as approving his quest to establish a fundamentalist Islamic state in Egypt. Shalabi firmly maintained that the Koran did no such thing. The breakdown came to a head during the Persian Gulf War (January 16–February 28, 1991), when a leaflet signed by Abdel-Rahman denounced Shalabi as a "bad Muslim."

In March 1991, Shalabi was found shot and stabbed to death in his apartment. Despite an investigation, police exhausted all leads and the case came to a dead end. Meanwhile, Sheik Abdel-Rhaman became the undisputed leader of the *jihad* office in Brooklyn.

"We Must Shake the Earth Under Their Feet"

2

The young Muslim men worshipping at the Al-Salam Mosque eagerly received Abdel-Rahman's message of vengeance. Their lives, tainted by disappointment or lack of opportunity, had prepared them to view the sheik's words favorably. "They're angry about poverty, inequality in wealth," the University of Chicago's Rashid Khalidi explained to *Newsweek* magazine in 1993. "They are people who are pretty angry at the rest of society."

In sermons that roared with indignation, the sheik powerfully expressed his disciples' rage and confusion. He drew them in with a call to action and a broad target—the United States itself. "Every conspiracy against Islam, every scheming against Islam and the Muslims—its source is America," he thundered. The chains around the Muslim heart were in plain sight, he said. America was the power behind Israel and behind Egypt's moderate President Hosni Mubarak. It was the reason why Muslims were forced to live in a state of humiliation and surrender, whether they resided in the run-down neighborhoods of Jersey City and Brooklyn, the slums of Cairo, or the alleys of Upper Egypt.

And yet, Abdel-Rahman declared, America itself lacked character and will, and its weaknesses stemmed from moral decay. A handful of faithful Muslims in the United States could not engage such a powerful enemy in open combat; that would be foolhardy, he preached. The way to victory was through a war of attrition, in which the enemy would be ground down by constant fear. Five or six small commando operations against the United States would force the powerful nation to run from international politics like a coward, abandoning its support for Israel and for other enemies of Islam.

While in prison, El Sayyid Nosair, the assassin of Meir Kahane, had been working out the details of an attack plan for crippling America from within its own borders. In June 1992, with Abdel-Rahman's blessing, Nosair's supporters traveled to Attica to hear his plan. Accompanying the well-wishers but unknown to them was Emad Salem, an FBI informant who had been planted in the *jihad* office during Nosair's trial. Salem had penetrated Abdel-Rahman's circle of trusted deputies so quickly that when Nosair laid out his plan, Salem was named a prominent participant.

The plan called for 12 pipe bombs to be planted at various targets: one aimed to assassinate the judge who had sentenced him, another to kill a Brooklyn assemblyman who had offended Muslims, and the other 10 for various Jewish-affiliated locations. Nosair's cousin, Ibrahim El-Gabrowney, would organize the attack, while FBI informant Emad Salem would direct the bomb construction.

To 25-year-old Mohammed Salameh, the former pupil of Abdullah Azzam, the plan sounded like a historic and glorious attack—and it was a blow he wanted to strike personally. Born in Palestine and raised in Jordan, Salameh had entered the United States in 1987 on a five-year visa and remained in the country illegally. "I am ready to work in America as a toilet cleaner or a garbage collector rather than stay here," he told his father before he left Jordan. Salameh's maternal grandfather fought in the 1936 Arab revolt against British rule in Palestine and was a member of the Palestine Liberation Organization (PLO); years later he was jailed by the Israelis. Salameh's maternal uncle, arrested in 1968 for terrorism, served 18 years in an Israeli prison before he was released and deported. In Iraq he was second in command in the "Western Sector," a PLO terrorist unit aided by the Iraqi government.

Now Salameh, part of a new generation of militants,

A man prays at the Al-Salam Mosque located in Jersey City, New Jersey, where Sheik Omar Abdel-Rahman preached to his followers, including several of the conspirators in the Trade Center bombing.

was being presented with a purpose, a cause that he could make his own. Perhaps because of his enthusiasm and willingness to volunteer, Nosair recognized in Salameh a fellow martyr. More likely, though, Nosair spotted a starry-eyed zealot who would serve as a scapegoat should the plans go awry.

On June 10, the newly recruited Salameh made the first of 46 phone calls to the Iraqi capital of Baghdad. Most of the calls were placed to his terrorist uncle, seeking advice and help. In six weeks, Salameh ran up a phone bill of more than $4,000 and lost his phone service—but not before reaching his contacts in Iraq to send "reinforcements" for the coming battle. On September 1, 1992, Salameh awaited the arrival of two experienced terrorists due that day at John F. Kennedy International Airport in New York City: Ramzi Yousef and Ahmad Ajaj.

To their fellow passengers on the flight to the United States, the two young men probably seemed unexceptional. Yousef wore a multicolored three-piece silk outfit, a fashionable way to dress in warmer parts of the world. Ajaj, who wore a conservative suit and tie, knew more about "looking American," having traveled to the United States for the first time a year earlier. After finding an apartment in Houston, Texas, he had filed a petition with the Immigration and Naturalization Service (INS) asking for political asylum. The Israeli government, he claimed, had imprisoned and tortured him for his peaceful opposition to the Israeli occupation of Palestine. An INS official listened to Ajaj's story and scheduled a hearing to review his petition.

Ajaj didn't bother to attend the hearing. Perhaps he only wanted to establish an identity on paper in the United States, believing it might some day be useful. In April 1992, Ajaj had left the United States under an assumed name. His destination was "Camp Khaldan," as the Central Intelligence Agency called it—a terrorist training center in Afghanistan, just across the border from Peshawar, Pakistan.

Ajaj first stopped in Saudi Arabia to pick up a letter of introduction, which he presented at Camp Khaldan. The letter requested that the camp's leader provide training in weapons and explosives for the bearer. Veterans at the camp welcomed the newcomer, and Ajaj soon settled into his lessons on constructing explosive devices.

Ajaj met Ramzi Yousef (which may not have been his real name) at the camp or through other acquaintances. An expert in Middle East terrorism believes that Iraqi agents supplied Yousef with a false identity by having him assume the credentials of a deceased man. Various reports record him either as a native of Iraq or Kuwait, educated in Swansea, Wales, and possibly raised in Pakistan. Yousef's reputation as a terrorist is traced to the Philippines, where he offered to help local Muslims manufacture bombs; he was nicknamed "the chemist" because of his skills. Before long, Yousef had a Filipino girlfriend, and the two were seen carousing in nightclubs and bars, contrary to the Islamic fundamentalist values he had vowed to defend by killing.

At Camp Khaldan, Ajaj and Yousef hit it off. They decided to apply their combined experience with explosives to targeting bombing sites in the United States. Ajaj amassed an extensive library of reference works about deadly devices, including a series of bomb-making manuals with blue covers. These "blue books," containing formulas for a number of explosive devices and materials, would later provide valuable information for the World Trade Center bombing conspirators. Judging from the handwritten notes in the blue books, Ajaj and Yousef focused on one particular kind of device that used the compound urea nitrite as its primary explosive. The instructions also outlined in detail a method of increasing the force of the bomb by adding ammonium nitrate dynamite, which is made using nitroglycerin.

Camp Khaldan also schooled its students in fabricating false identification documents. Ajaj and Yousef dutifully collected photographs, various ID cards, bank records, education records, and medical records belonging to other people to create the IDs they would use to enter the United States. Finally, the two watched videotapes that not only demonstrated how to make explosives but also advocated a specific bombing target—the United States. The opening scene in one of the videos shows a van crashing into the front of a U.S. embassy. Once inside the embassy, the driver—bent not only on killing others but also on becoming a martyr for the cause—detonates a bomb, destroying the embassy.

Ajaj assembled his collection in a traveling kit—two notebooks with handwritten notes on explosives, six blue books or bomb-making manuals, two instructional videotapes on making explosives, anti-American and anti-Israeli materials, and documents proving false identities—everything he needed to successfully complete a terrorist expedition. In August 1992, shortly after Salameh's phone-calling spree, Ajaj and Yousef used assumed names to book reservations on a flight from Pakistan to New York City.

On August 31, the men boarded a flight from Peshawar to Karachi and sat together in first class. In Karachi, where they changed planes, they checked in separately and sat apart from one another to disguise the fact that they were traveling together. When they arrived in New York, they made it through customs screenings by showing phony passports—Yousef a British one and Ajaj a Swedish one. Since visitors entering the United States on Swedish passports do not even need a visa, Ajaj expected no trouble, so he carried the kit.

The INS inspector at the customs desk noticed that Ajaj's passport had been altered—his photograph had been affixed on top of the original photo—so he told Ajaj to step into a secondary inspection area. In Ajaj's luggage, according to federal prosecutors, the inspector discovered "formulae regarding how to destroy buildings, bridges, and other properties, and videotapes which called for war on the United States and portrayed scenes of explosions, including depictions of American facilities being bombed." The inspector called for assistance and questioned Ajaj about the contents of his luggage. Watching calmly from the line at the next counter, Yousef pretended he was simply another observer. Customs agents led Ajaj away.

Now it was Yousef's turn at the counter. Perhaps

A satellite photograph of the Zhawar Kili support complex in Afghanistan, a training ground for terrorists. Ramzi Yousef and Ahmad Ajaj both received expert training at a camp similar to this one before immigrating to the United States.

Ahmad Ajaj, who arrived in the United States with fellow conspirator Ramzi Yousef, was an explosives expert whose extensive notes on making bombs proved invaluable to the terrorist team.

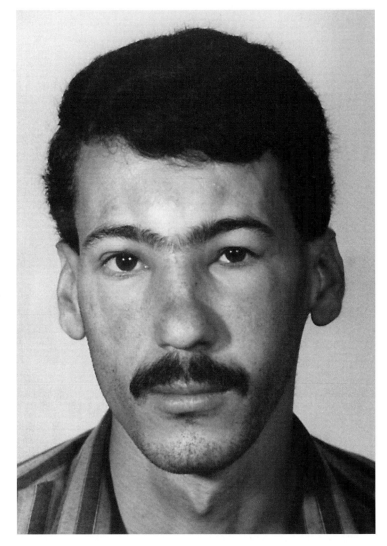

seeing Ajaj's misfortune, he opted to produce a more believable Iraqi passport instead of a British one. The inspector glanced at the passport and then also directed Yousef to the secondary inspection area, where he was promptly taken into custody for not having a valid visa to enter the United States. Escorted to the INS office in the airport for questioning, Yousef, a quick thinker, apologized and asked for help. He admitted he had improperly boarded the flight to New York by bribing an official in

Pakistan. He needed political asylum, he explained. The Iraqi military had tortured him. He was traveling alone and didn't know whom to ask for help. INS officials told him to sign a statement declaring that he was applying for asylum. Then they fingerprinted him, and he was released on his own recognizance pending a hearing. He expressed his gratitude and went his way, confident there was time enough now to complete his mission.

Yousef did not know it, but he was the beneficiary of even more good fortune. Two months earlier, the FBI had cut off contact with Emad Salem, its informant in the *jihad* office. Persistent rumors had circulated that Salem was in the pay of the Egyptian government.

Moreover, he had refused to follow official procedures relating to criminal investigations. As a result of the FBI cutoff, information about Abdel-Rahman and his inner circle had dried up around the time Nosair's bombing plot had turned into a plan to destroy the World Trade Center.

Within two days of Yousef's arrival in the United States, he contacted Mohammed Salameh and another man named Musab Yasin, both of whom lived in the same building in Jersey City, New Jersey. The apartment building was an address used by many young Arab men who often ate and prayed together; an intercom linked their apartments. A few days after Yousef moved in, Musab's older brother, Abdul Yasin, arrived from Baghdad. Yousef took the young Salameh under his wing, and in October the two moved to another address in Jersey City, where they shared a rented room.

Two others joined the group of conspirators around this time. The first was Nidal Ayyad, a naturalized citizen from Kuwait who had achieved the American Dream, according to his proud relatives, and had graduated from Rutgers University with a degree in chemical engineering. Ayyad worked for Allied Signal Corporation, and his mother had arranged for him to marry a Middle Eastern woman. The other was tall, red-haired Mahmud Abouhalima who had served as an assistant to Mustafa Shalabi, Abdel-Rahman's rival at the *jihad* office until his murder in 1991. Abouhalima, who would become the conspirators' adviser on the "outside," had come to the United States via Germany under permanent alien status as a "farmworker," even though he was now a New York City cab driver. He had been Abdel-Rahman's personal driver as well, and police strongly suspected him of having a hand in the murder of Shalabi.

The conspirators' first task was to obtain materials for the bomb, a purchase that required a large amount of cash. Almost $10,000 was immediately wired from a mysterious overseas source that the FBI was never able to pinpoint. With the money, Salameh and Ayyad opened a joint bank account at the National Westminster Bank branch in Jersey City, a few blocks from the Al-Salam Mosque where Abdel-Rahman's followers worshipped. A week later, the two men withdrew the money from the account and transferred it to an individual bank account opened by Salameh that day. In early November, they placed several calls to chemical companies. Yousef also began contacting surgical supply companies about gloves, masks, and rubber tubing, all of which he'd need to construct the bomb. Before long, however, they realized that the bomb they hoped to build was too expensive, so they scaled back the quantities of materials. Because some of the more volatile ingredients could not be stored safely for long periods, the bombers also moved up their target date to late February. Although INS officials had confiscated Ajaj's blue books during his arrest at the airport (Ajaj was serving a six-month sentence for being a danger to U.S. interests), the conspirators still believed they could achieve their goal using Yousef's knowledge.

Nidal Ayyad joined the World Trade Center conspirators in late 1992, and as a chemical engineer brought his technical expertise to making a bomb capable of toppling the twin towers.

From City Chemical Corporation, Yousef ordered delivery of 1,000 pounds of technical-grade urea and 105 gallons of nitric acid to make urea nitrate for the bomb's main charge. He also purchased 60 gallons of sulfuric acid, packaged in 15-gallon carboys (rectangular cushioned glass, plastic, or metal containers for liquids). These were for the nitroglycerin to be used for boosters. He also ordered a gallon of ethyl alcohol, which would stabilize the nitroglycerin for transport; and a 25-pound bag of sodium carbonate to neutralize acids during the mixing process. For all of these purchases Yousef paid cash. In mid-December, Abouhalima, who was now in daily phone contact with Salameh and Yousef, purchased a 16-ounce can of smokeless powder for detonators.

Salameh rented a storage shed at the Space Station Storage Company in Jersey City, where they had all of the bomb-making materials delivered or deposited. Yousef, Salameh, Ayyad, and Abouhalima had now reached a crossroads. They needed Ajaj's blue books to mix the bomb ingredients. The main explosive would be a kind of gloppy substance that was placed in plastic bags, but one false move—creating sparks by scuffing a shoe on a carpet, or combining volatile substances incorrectly—could cause the conspirators themselves to be vaporized in seconds.

On December 4, 1992, a few days after Yousef ordered the first shipment of supplies from City Chemical, he placed a series of calls to Ajaj's lawyer in New York and to a friend of Ajaj's in Texas. On December 29, Ajaj returned the call from prison, patched through to Yousef by the friend in a three-way call. Knowing their conversation was probably being monitored by prison officials, Ajaj and Yousef spoke in Arabic and in code. Ajaj told Yousef that the court had ordered the government to return his belongings. Yousef asked whether he should pick up Ajaj's things, and Ajaj commented that it was not smart for Yousef himself to pick up the materials from the government because it might jeopardize Yousef's "business," which would be "a pity," Ajaj said. Send someone else, he suggested. Eventually, the bombers recovered the blue books and set to work building their bomb.

Meanwhile Yousef, an experienced terrorist, began planning his escape route. On November 9, he had reported the loss of his passport to Jersey City police and claimed to be Abdul Basit Mahmud Abdul Karim, a Pakistani born and reared in Kuwait. From December 3 to 27, Yousef made a number of calls to Baluchistan in Iran. Records of these calls later gave investigators a map of Yousef's escape route—through Pakistan and Baluchistan, across the Arabian Sea to Oman, where the "telephone trail" ended.

On December 31, armed with photocopies of current and previous passports belonging to Abdul Basit, Yousef appeared at the Pakistani consulate in New York and repeated his story about having lost his passport. He offered his records as proof that he was indeed Abdul Basit. The consulate officials fingered his photocopies suspiciously and denied him a new permanent passport. But they did grant him a six-month temporary passport and told him to straighten things out when he returned "home." Yousef was satisfied with the temporary document. After all, it would get him on a plane after blowing up the World Trade Center. That was enough.

With the blue books and most of the chemicals in hand, the bomb construction went into high gear. In January 1993, Abouhalima helped Yousef and Salameh move into another Jersey City apartment. There, at 40 Pamrapo Avenue, a building set back from the street to provide seclusion, they built the bomb. They made sure to get a ground floor unit to allow quick escape, as Ajaj's manuals recommended.

Sheik Abdel-Rahman could hardly conceal his excitement over the catastrophe unfolding. That month he delivered a speech in Brooklyn forecasting the carnage that would soon follow. America, he railed, is the foremost enemy of Islam. Muslims "must be terrorists and we must terrorize the enemies of Islam and frighten them and disturb them and shake the earth under their feet." Abdel-Rahman even consented to an interview with *Newsweek* reporter Tom Masland, who asked the sheik whether he had issued *fatwas* approving violent activities and attacks on tourists. "Did anybody intercept any kind of a letter or any kind of written statement or anything else [made by me]?" Abdel-Rahman asked in return. "I'm asking: what is the clue that they have based their accusation on?" The reason the United States wanted to deport him, Abdel-Rahman continued, was because "I am preaching and calling for the freedom of the people back in Egypt and all over the Muslim world. I'm certain that I didn't break the law in the United States." Why had he settled in the United States? the reporter asked. "I go anywhere for the word of Allah. This is my ultimate duty, to preach for Islam. I invite you, yourself, to be a Muslim," he said.

At the bomb-making factory, meanwhile, the conspirators were learning that mixing the bomb's ingredients was a nasty business, even when they followed the directions in one of Ajaj's manuals, titled "Rapid Destruction and Demolition." First they had to dissolve urea nitrate in water and then add nitric acid, creating harsh fumes that required them to wear surgical masks. The fumes were so strong that they turned some of the paint on the walls from white to blue and corroded the inside of one of the apartment's doorknobs and a set of door hinges. At one point the urea nitrate overheated and bubbled, splattering the walls and hitting the ceiling of the back bedroom. The conspirators also flushed some of the excess chemicals down the toilet, spilling urea nitrate on the bathroom floor.

They added aluminum powder and other metals to enhance the urea nitrate mixture and to increase the bomb's destructive impact. They mixed another explosive substance, nitroglycerin, and created sticks of ammonium nitrate dynamite, which they wrapped in duct tape and added to the bomb as boosters. They spilled nitroglycerin on themselves and in the apartment during the process. Then, as portions of the explosives were mixed to a thick consistency, the conspirators transported them in plastic bags to a shed in the Space Station storage facility, where

After the bombing, FBI investigators enter the apartment of Ramzi Yousef and Mohammed Salameh in Jersey City. There the FBI would find conclusive evidence that the terrorist group had met and planned its attack at this site.

the bomb remained until they had a vehicle to transport it to the World Trade Center.

Would the bomb be big enough? They thought about the size of the target—a 16-acre complex, 110 stories high, occupied by roughly 20,000 employees and 30,000 shoppers, businesspeople, and commuters. They decided it was better to overdo it and planned for even more explosive power. Ayyad, the chemical engineer, suggested using hydrogen gas to intensify the power of the bomb. Yousef wanted to add cyanide gas—it would multiply the death toll by poisoning many hundreds of people, he explained—

but the cost was out of the question. Ayyad approached his employer, Allied Signal Corporation, for cylinders of hydrogen gas, but he was refused. Then he called a number of compressed gas companies from his office telephone, and even used company stationery to fax his purchase orders. Finally, he found AGL Welding Supply Company, which promised to deliver the hydrogen gas to the storage shed.

Once the conspirators finished preparing the bomb, they began scouting their target. In mid-February, Ayyad rented a car and listed Salameh as an additional driver. Salameh drove the car to inspect the B-2 garage level of the World Trade Center. As its name suggests, the B-2 level is the second underground level of six; it is used primarily for parking. The U.S. Secret Service kept a fleet of cars there, fenced off from the larger public parking area. Salameh selected a spot for the bomb just inside the garage, between the twin towers, consistent with the plan to make the towers crash into each other.

On February 21, less than a week before the bombing, a latecomer to the conspiracy arrived from Dallas—a Palestinian named Eyyad Ismoil, who had been a high school classmate of Yousef's in Kuwait. Why Ismoil joined the conspiracy so late in the plan is unclear. Perhaps the conspirators needed someone to transport the bomb to its target. Ayyad exchanged the first rental car for a different one, probably to avoid suspicion, and again listed Salameh as an additional driver. Two days before the bombing the conspirators once again checked out the B-2 level of the World Trade Center.

On Tuesday, February 23, Salameh rented a yellow Ford Econoline van from a Ryder agency in Jersey City. The van was the largest vehicle that would not only fit in the low overhead of the parking garage but would also carry the 1,500 pounds of explosives they had manufactured. Salameh told the Ryder agent he needed the van until at least the 28th, and he placed a $400 deposit on it. Two days later, a delivery truck from AGL Welding arrived at the Space Station facility with Ayyad's order of hydrogen tanks. But as the AGL driver attempted to unload the tanks, an employee of the storage facility stopped him. Hydrogen tanks were prohibited in the shed because of their explosive potential. After Salameh assured him that a van was on its way to pick up the hydrogen tanks, the employee relented. A short while later, Salameh and Yousef hoisted the tanks into the rented Ryder van, then drove away.

On Thursday—the day before the bombing—the conspirators transferred all the explosives into the van. That night, Salameh took steps to prevent being associated with the rented van. He falsely reported it to the police as stolen and deliberately provided an incorrect license plate number, hoping to throw them off his trail. He discovered, however, that without the correct information, the police could not register a stolen vehicle report.

Early on Friday, February 26, a cold, overcast day with snow flurries in New York, the conspirators gathered at a Shell gas station in New Jersey. There they topped off the gas tank—one last explosive touch—before heading into Manhattan. With Ismoil at the wheel, they drove to the World Trade Center, parked the van on the B-2 level of the garage, set the bomb to detonate in the middle of the busy workday, and fled the scene.

"We're Going to Make It! We're Going to Make It!"

A schoolteacher leads her terrified charges away from the chaotic scene at the World Trade Center. The explosion had trapped the class on an elevator around the 107th floor of the tower for over four hours.

3

At a quarter past noon on Friday, February 26, 17 kindergartners from Public School No. 95 in Brooklyn completed their tour of the World Trade Center's observation deck. Teacher Anna Marie Tesoriero ushered the children into the elevator on the 107th floor, and the doors closed. As the elevator descended, the kids watched the lighted display panel and loudly called off the numbers of the floors.

Far below in the basement cafeteria, refrigerator mechanic Joseph Cacciatore glanced at the clock while on his lunch break. Seconds later, the bomb planted inside the Ford Econoline van on level B-2 detonated. The force of the concussion blew out Cacciatore's contact lenses and shattered one of his eye sockets.

In an office 30 feet from the van, a 3,000-pound steel beam hurtled through the wall like a giant javelin, killing four people—a locksmith, an engineer, an operations superintendent, and a pregnant secretary. In the B-2 level stairway, a steel door tore off its hinges and embedded itself in a concrete wall 35 feet away. The lobby windows of the complex blew out onto the plaza as huge marble slabs fell and shattered.

Cacciatore felt his face, which was sticky with blood. Around him people were screaming "God help us!" as 2,500 tons of concrete crashed down through levels B-2, B-3, B-4, and B-5, crushing electrical and refrigeration equipment as it fell, and killing a dental equipment salesman looking for his car in the parking garage. The concrete slabs slammed onto the floor of B-6, the lowest basement level of the building, raining debris on the platform of the subway station beneath the World Trade Center. High above, the elevator carrying the kindergartners from P.S. 95 abruptly jerked to a halt between floors 35 and 36. The colored lights in the ceiling went out, leaving the car in the dark of the elevator shaft.

All over New York City, television programs whose stations had transmitters atop the World Trade Center winked off the air. Lights in the huge seven-building complex flickered, dimmed, and went out. Ruptured plumbing spewed a torrent of water in a cascade, through the blast hole and all the way to the bottom of building. On the street, passersby saw the twin 110-story towers sway in the wintry air, as the force of the explosion shuddered upward.

On the 37th floor, Joseph Gibney, a disabled federal attorney confined to a wheelchair, stopped talking on the phone and paused in mid-bite of a slice of pizza when someone shouted, "What the hell was that?" Then his phone went dead, the computers shut down, and the entire office clattered and shook. On the 35th floor, Charles Maikish, the director of complex, paused in the middle of signing a lease, feeling a "slight lifting of the tower." Maikish dropped the lease, ran to a paralyzed elevator, unlocked it with a special fire department key, and descended to the ground floor, anxious to find out what was happening.

More than 200 cars, including 50 Secret Service vehicles, had instantly combusted on level B-2, releasing a caustic, oily smoke. Stairwells and the elevator shafts of the World Trade Center's 99 elevators acted as chimneys and sucked the smoke upward. Some of the smoke filtered into the darkened and stalled elevator cars, where passengers waited nervously for instructions that never arrived. On the 105th floor, David Deshane "saw smoke everywhere" and ran to the fire emergency button. He hit it several times with the heel of his hand, but nothing happened.

From a spot across the Hudson River on the New Jersey waterfront, Ramzi Yousef savored the sight of the black plumes of smoke curling from the tops of the towers. His five-month mission to the United States was completed.

In their elevator car the kindergartners smelled smoke, but the adults reassured them that everything would be all right. "Let's sing the theme song from *Barney*," Marie Tesoriero suggested. As the kids began to sing, she quietly took from her purse a rosary, and—not knowing whether anyone knew where they were—prepared to lead the children in prayer.

On the 43rd floor, an accountant almost seven months pregnant named Geralyn Hearne also smelled acrid fumes. She told her friend Donna Anderson that the odor was making her feel sick, and then suddenly went into a seizure. Anderson held her friend in her arms and tried to make her comfortable. "If we don't get her out of here, she could die," Anderson thought.

Across the street from the World Trade Center, the city's Fire Department Engine Company 10 radioed headquarters that it had just received a call of a possible transformer vault explosion in the towers. Red and yellow emergency vehicles rolled out the doors into the street with sirens blaring.

Inside the World Trade Center, chaos reigned. Phones were dead, and the emergency backup network for the complex's lighting, alarm, and speaker systems was down. Aware that in emergencies one should avoid elevators, some office workers headed for stairwells. Many headed down the stairs regardless of the darkness and smoke. On the 37th floor, two of Gibney's colleagues lifted him out of his wheelchair and started carrying him down to the lobby. Gibney could feel both men struggling. The smoke thickened as they descended. One of his rescuers staggered and nearly fell. A young Asian man took over for him and urged them on, shouting, "We're going to make it! We're going to make it!" On the ground floor they joined the hundreds of others who spilled out of the building into the plaza through the hot spray from ruptured steam pipes. Many were coughing and gasping for air. Others had been bloodied from the blast.

The New York police and fire departments soon realized that a major catastrophe was unfolding. All 18 lines connected to the 911 emergency number were tied up. Within three minutes of the explosion, callers were reporting smoke in the towers as far up as the 33rd floor. Others reported that the ceiling had collapsed in the subway station. Calls came in so quickly from cell phones of people stranded in the tower that operators directed them to call one of the central offices of the five city boroughs.

Within minutes, the disaster went to 16 alarms, the highest alarm level in New York City history. Sixty-six fire engines, 52 fire trucks, five rescue companies, and two fireboats (on the Hudson River) arrived to help. Still, the torrent of calls to police and fire stations continued. Fire

professionals advised people in the towers to stay put, cover all air vents, and stay calm. They advised them not to break windows, because the draft it created would draw smoke inside. Adding to the confusion, however, was a newscaster for the only TV station that remained on the air. Workers who watched the report on portable televisions inside the building were told to smash their office windows. Showers of broken glass rained down on the 500 emergency personnel trying to enter the buildings and caused more injuries.

Hundreds of police, medical, and fire rescue vehicles arrive on the scene after the Trade Center explosion. Emergency response to the disaster eventually reached the 16-alarm level, the highest in New York City history.

Office workers awaiting rescue stand by broken windows. Minutes after the explosion, callers from the upper floors reported seeing smoke.

On the 43rd floor, Donna Anderson tended to Geralyn Hearne as best she could until firefighters stormed in and helped the stricken woman to a chair, then lifted it down the stairs. As they passed the elevators, Anderson heard screaming from inside the shafts.

On the ground, firefighters quickly pinpointed the source of the smoke. Kevin Shea of New York Fire Department's Rescue Company No. 1 donned a face mask, dove into the billowing smoke, and inched his way across the B-2 garage. Suddenly, the floor buckled under him and sent him headlong into the crater created by the blast. He crashed into a pile of office dividers and broke his left knee and right foot. The impact tore off his helmet and face mask. Shea used his arms to shield his face from rocks and cinders dropping from the crater's edge. "This is it," he thought, believing he would be killed. "Please God," he prayed, "take me quick."

To emergency management officials, it seemed as if circumstances were conspiring against them. Fog blanketing the area turned radio and TV antennas on the roof of the 110th floor into a deadly steel forest, preventing helicopter rescue. Firefighters shouted vainly into their low-wattage radios, not realizing that the equipment wasn't powerful enough to penetrate dozens of concrete floors. Volunteer emergency teams of office workers tried to help, but they hadn't been trained on what to do if the public address system didn't work. Office workers trapped on the upper floors tried several times to descend the stairs, but even the emergency lighting was out, and the dark, smoke-filled stairwells seemed like an invitation to death.

At 1:35 P.M., a caller to the New York Police Department claimed credit for the explosion. "The blast is no accident," the caller warned. He identified himself as a member of the Serbian Liberation Front. At 2:15 P.M., a second caller declared that a bomb had been placed in the Empire State Building. Police immediately evacuated that building, although no bombs were discovered. In the next 24 hours, 19 calls claiming credit for the World Trade Center bombing came through.

Firefighters spent the rest of the afternoon and evening trying to get everyone out of the World Trade Center buildings. At the site of the bomb, Lt. Joe Ward found Kevin Shea and, with the help of other firefighters, hoisted him out of the crater to safety. One of the firefighters later told reporters that the glow from the burning explosives made the crater seem "like a giant barbecue pit with coals burning."

Eight people trapped in an elevator near the 57th floor spent three hours chiseling through a sheetrock wall with a single car key. Among them was Eugene Fasullo, chief engineer for the Port Authority of New York and New Jersey, the owner of the tower complex. Once free, he hurried to join director Charles Maikish and a crew of Port Authority engineers who had set up a makeshift command center in the ballroom of the Vista Hotel. Within an hour of the blast, while dozens of fires still burned, Port Authority engineers ventured out to assess the damage.

At St. Vincent's hospital, doctors performed a Caesarian section on Geralyn Hearne and delivered a baby girl two months prematurely. Firefighters worked all afternoon, floor by floor, as emergency operators fielded calls from friends and relatives seeking news of loved ones who might have been caught in the explosion. At about 5:00 P.M., the Brooklyn kindergartners and their teacher heard a shout telling them to stand back from the walls of the elevator. A light appeared and firefighters broke through. The group finally reached the ground floor, where an anguished school bus driver waited to take them home.

Just a few hours after the explosion and across town, Mohammed Salameh, confident that the Ryder van had been blown to bits, showed up at the Jersey City rental agency claiming that the vehicle had been stolen and asking for his $400 security deposit back. The rental agent explained that he needed to file a police report and then return with a copy of it. Salameh, who had deliberately given police the wrong license plate number the day before and was refused a police report, left in disgust.

News of the bombing in New York sent federal law enforcement agencies into a Code Red alert, the highest state of readiness. The FBI established an emergency command center in Washington, D.C., where director William Sessions spent most of the day commanding the FBI's Terrorist Task Force. The Bureau of Alcohol, Tobacco, and Firearms (ATF)—the agency responsible for investigating the illegal use of explosives—mobilized its Bomber National Response Team.

In news reports, New York Governor Mario Cuomo declared, "It looks like a bomb, it smells like a bomb, it's probably a bomb." The bombers themselves, however, were disappointed. They had had visions of the twin towers being sawed from their bases by the explosion, tumbling into Manhattan's financial center like double iron hammers, crushing the life out of a quarter of a million people. That evening, Salameh drove Yousef and Eyyad Ismoil to John F. Kennedy International Airport. He had contacted the police again, explaining that he needed a copy of the stolen vehicle report to show the Ryder agency, and was told once more that he needed the correct license plate number. Now, without the deposit money, Salameh watched as Yousef and Ismoil boarded a Pakistani International Airlines flight to Karachi. Yousef, using falsified documents, would proceed to Quetta, Pakistan, near the Afghanistan border; Ismoil would fly home to Jordan.

Before departing, Yousef gave Salameh a plane ticket to Amsterdam on Royal Jordanian Flight 262, continuing to Amman, Jordan. The ticket, dated March 5, would allow Salameh to acquire a Dutch visa. Sometime in the next two days, however, Salameh discovered the truth about his ticket—it was a $65 infant's fare. Mahmud Abouhalima, the cab driver and "outside man" on the

New York City police officers stand around the blast hole created by the explosion in the building's garage. Following the disaster, rescue workers would reconstruct supports for some of the building's blasted columns.

plan, later suspected that Yousef had deliberately used Salameh and Nidal Ayyad, the chemical engineer, as "bait" for federal agents. While Yousef put distance between himself and the bombing, agents would spend time tracking down, arresting, and interrogating the two men. Said Abouhalima, "Yousef used [them] . . . as pawns."

At approximately 11:25 P.M. that night, less than one-half hour after Yousef's flight took off, firefighters in the World Trade Center located the final damaged elevator. Its occupants, trapped for 12 hours, staggered to medical trucks to be examined. Officials declared the incident under control at 2:25 A.M. on Saturday, February 27th. By early evening on February 28th, Port Authority chief engineer Eugene Fasullo and his team produced a preliminary report. Some of the structural columns that held up the Visa Hotel had been severely weakened. In addition, the explosion had demolished floor slabs, leaving the columns naked and unstable with little support. The ruined slabs now lay three floors below in a debris pile 12 feet deep.

Mohammed Salameh, now stranded in "enemy" territory without enough money, absolutely had to get the deposit money back on the van.

A week after the explosion, a member of the FBI terrorist task force gathers clues from the World Trade Center bombing wreckage. Investigators had to make a long, detailed analysis of the wreck before they could draw any conclusions about the bomb's composition.

"We Have to Be Sherlock Holmes"

4

By Saturday, February 27th, the day after the bombing, the names of the dead or presumed dead were known: Monica Smith, a pregnant secretary; Wilfredo Mercado, a restaurant worker; Steven Knapp, a maintenance supervisor; William Macko, a maintenance worker; Robert Kirkpatrick, a locksmith; and John DiGiovanni, a dental salesman. Mercado's body was buried under tons of rubble and would not be found until two weeks later. Medical examiners noted that the intensity of the blast had stamped the pattern of Monica Smith's sweater on her shoulder.

The media scrambled to inform the public about the bombing, but because state and federal officials admitted that it was too early to tell what had really occurred, rumors became headlines instead. Experts speculated that the bomb consisted of 500 to 1,000 pounds of C-4 plastic (meaning pliable or moldable) explosive, but they theorized that other types of explosives, such as Semtex, dynamite, TNT, or fertilizer mixed with fuel oil, could cause a similar level of destruction. News reports said that it was believed the bomb arrived in a van, a panel truck, or a Ford Bronco. The bombers might have been Serbs, Iraqis, Palestinians, or a South American drug cartel, since members of all of these groups held political grudges against the United States. Everyone wanted to know where the bombers were now. Many believed—or hoped—they were buried in the bottom of the blast hole.

Some political and ethnic groups reacted angrily to being affiliated in the press with the bombers. Responding to news reports that a caller from the Serbian Liberation Front had claimed credit for the attack, George Bogdanich, a spokesman for a coalition of Serbian-American groups, retorted, "Any fool can pick up a telephone and claim anything." The American Muslim Council issued a statement declaring that it was wrong to "paint the incident as an act of Muslim terrorism."

Jerry Bremer, the top antiterrorism official in the U.S. State Department during the 1980s, agreed that jumping to conclusions was unwise. "We shouldn't automatically [assume] this is the beginning of a new world war," he said. "It's entirely possible that this is some disgruntled employee who's been fired." Nevertheless, another State Department official warned ominously, "If the FBI can link this to a foreign government, rest assured the price will be paid."

Speculation ended within 48 hours after the explosion, however. The conspirators themselves turned out to be eager to let the world know who they were. On Saturday, Nidal Ayyad called the *New York Daily News* "tip line." In his spoken message, which the newspaper recorded, Ayyad proclaimed: "This is the Liberation Army. We conducted the explosion at the World Trade Center. You will get our demands by mail. This is the Liberation Army."

The call, which was one of many being received by news outlets and law enforcement officials, might simply have been added to the growing log of misleading or crank calls coming in about the bombing. However, this caller had said something different from any of the others: he had promised that a letter of demands would be forthcoming. He was right—on Monday, three days after the bombing, a letter written in awkward English arrived at the *New York Times* offices. It read:

> We are, the fifth battalion in the LIBERATION ARMY, declare our responsibility for the explosion on the mentioned building. This action was done in response for the American political, economical, and military support to Israel the state of terrorism and to the rest of the dictator countries in the region.
>
> OUR DEMANDS ARE:
> 1 Stop all military, economical, and political aid to Israel.
> 2 All diplomatic relations with Israel must stop.
> 3 Not to interfere with any of the Middle East countries interior affairs.
>
> IF our demands are not met, all of our functional groups in the army will continue to execute our missions against the military and civilian targets in and out the United States. . . . The terrorism that Israel practices (Which is supported by America) must be faced with a similar one. The dictatorship and terrorism (also supported by America) that some countries are practicing against their own people must also be faced with terrorism. . . . The American people are responsible for the actions of their government and they must question all of the

crimes that their government is committing against other people. Or they—Americans—will be the targets of our operations that could diminish them.

[signed]

LIBERATION ARMY
FIFTH BATTALION

Of course, the handful of conspirators were not an army or even an organized military unit. The five men involved were no doubt attempting to make themselves seem more fearsome, given what they believed was a disappointing outcome to their plan. In a second, undelivered draft of the letter, which was later recovered from Ayyad's computer by law enforcement officials, the group admitted that the World Trade Center bomb did not cause as much damage as they had hoped. They warned, however, that they would be more precise in the future and would continue to target the World Trade Center if their demands were not met.

Meanwhile, investigators were on the bomb site assessing the damage. As they picked through the rubble in the basement, they realized that although the building presented a very visible and symbolic target, it was structurally a poor choice for mass destruction. Charles Maikish, the director of the complex who had felt the tower "lift" at the instant of the explosion, later proudly told *Popular Mechanics* magazine, "No other structure, no complex would have withstood that kind of blast."

In designing the towers, architect Minoru Yamasaki had planned for the worst. Twenty-one steel columns spaced 10 feet apart and braced with horizontal beams formed the exterior frame of the towers when they were constructed. These "steel curtain walls" supply strength, but they also provide flexibility: in heavy winds, each of the World Trade Center towers can sway up to three feet without damage, even in blasts of wind greater than 150 mph. Had the bomb sliced through 10 columns in one tower alone, the structure still would not have collapsed. In fact, the instruments recording wind sway in the World Trade Center registered nothing unusual from the exploding truck on level B-2.

No doubt the bombers thought that placing the truck in the reinforced enclosure of the garage was a wise move. They probably assumed that containing the blast in such an enclosure would increase its power by doubling the force of the shock waves, transmitting it directly to the structure. They were wrong. Instead, the 12-inch concrete floor slabs in the six-level basement acted as blast shields. When the bomb exploded, five of the slabs—two above and three below—were pulverized, but the energy had been dispersed. This limited the force of the bomb, creating only a 200- by 100-foot hole through the five affected levels.

Still, as investigators entered the garage area and the "blast seat" (the center of the explosion) on Saturday morning, they saw an other worldly scene. Blackened and twisted cars lay in heaps, their frames still smoking; theft alarms from other vehicles bleated weakly. One hundred twenty-four vehicles were destroyed, including 50 Secret Service cars. From the ceilings, loops of cables and conduits hung everywhere. Around the 11,500 square-foot blast hole, massive chunks of concrete were suspended in midair from bent ropes of rebar (steel rods used to reinforce concrete). On level B-6, the very bottom of the hole, 200,000 cubic feet of water stood 1.5 feet deep, fed by gushing sewer and water lines, steam pipes, and seven 7,000-ton refrigeration units that were crushed beneath 2,500 tons of concrete. When they aimed their flashlights upward, investigators could see the hole punched through the floor of the Vista Hotel ballroom. Below the base of the building, under the basement levels, partition walls had blown out onto the platform and rails of the subway station, knocking out commuter service between Manhattan and New Jersey for days.

Once area hospitals had checked in with officials, the media reported the final human toll. Six people had been killed and 1,000 had been injured, including 105 firefighters and rescuers. Officials estimated the cost of repairing the physical damage to the World Trade Center at hundreds of millions of dollars. At the White House, President Bill Clinton monitored the investigation from a temporary "war room" set up specifically to address the disaster. During his weekly Saturday radio address the day after the explosion, the president assured Americans of intense federal efforts to catch the bombers. "Americans should know we'll do everything in our power to keep them safe in their streets, their offices, and their homes," he declared.

Already the FBI had transferred state-of-the art forensics equipment to the lab of the New York Police Department (NYPD) on East 20th Street in Manhattan. Before investigators could safely enter the blast site, however, workers had to buttress the sagging remnants of the garage and lay down a web of tubular steel beams across the bomb crater. "We need to get into the crater to solve this thing," an impatient Police Commissioner Raymond Kelly said, "and we can't get in until the site has been shored up." Finally, after several hours of work, members of the NYPD bomb squad were lowered by rope into the crater. There, they used foot-long cotton swabs to obtain the first samples of bomb residue.

Privately, crime scene investigators expected a long and complex process. Said one federal official, "The forensic challenge is tremendous. We have to worry about structural engineering—we don't want the World Trade Center to fall on top of us. We have to worry about

Nearly three weeks after the explosion, Port Authority workers were still checking for bodies beneath the rubble. Workers found the body of Wilfredo Mercado, the final identified victim, two weeks after the disaster.

archeology—how to move massive amounts of material without losing microscopic evidence. And we have to be Sherlock Holmes."

The first question was: What was the bomb made of? Most well-known terrorist groups have their own bomb "signatures"; that is, they use characteristic explosive compounds, detonators, and even device designs. Sophisticated plastic explosives tend to shred metal and pulverize concrete, for example, while common substances such as dynamite usually knock over walls and shove vehicles around. Once the explosive substance could be identified, investigators could determine next whether the bomb was a homemade explosive constructed from commercially available material or a product of limited availability, such as a military-grade explosive. Investigators hoped that the materials would prove to be the latter—that they were made of scarce substances not easily purchased. In that case, the bombers' identities would be much easier to determine.

The second question was: Where were the bombers? Had they been killed in the blast? The explosion appeared to have occurred at the foot of the B-2 ramp, not in a specific parking space. Maybe, investigators thought, the bombers had hit a speed bump, which triggered a premature explosion. They used specially trained police dogs to sniff at the rubble and pick up what might have been the scent of human bodies.

The FBI's Rapid Start Team of computer specialists and information technicians also got down to business, processing and collating thousands of pieces of data about the blast. FBI field officers were notified to search for clues, including bits of physical evidence, possible leads on bombers' identities, rumors, witness reports—whatever might help solve the crime. The search spread around the world. Alerts were circulated to foreign law enforcement agencies, and the international law enforcement agency Interpol combed its records for parallels to the style and methods used in the World Trade Center attack. FBI legal attachés in U.S. embassies were told to begin amassing information on overseas terrorism as well.

An immediate practical problem was where to store the physical evidence—car parts, glass, shredded metal, and so on—coming out of the blast site. FBI investigators

scouted Manhattan's financial district for a space large enough to handle all the items. They planned to avert the usual but tedious process of piecing objects together to find clues. Instead, they decided, after they knew the nature of the bomb from chemical residues at the site, they would build scale models of the garage and then explode them. The resulting data were fed into computers. All they knew for sure at that point was that the blast was so massive that a truck or van must have been used to carry the bomb. A car would have been too small to carry an explosive of that size and strength.

And then an extraordinary piece of luck fell into investigators' laps. On Sunday evening, two days after the explosion, 10 investigators—8 from the ATF and 2 from

Workers and investigators go over the Trade Center's architectural plans, trying to determine the extent of damage to the building's support system.

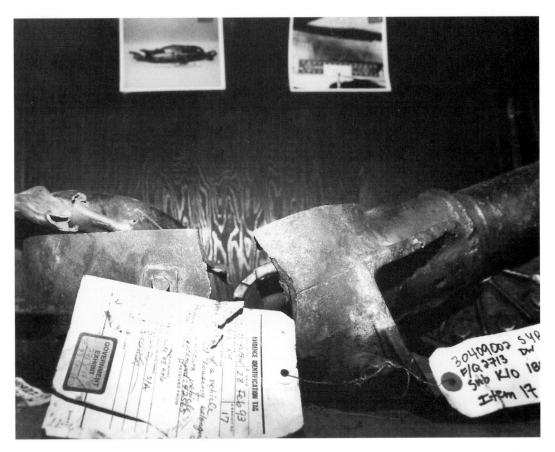

FBI investigators eventually discovered these charred remnants of the Ryder truck van that had held the deadly bomb. A vehicle identification number etched under the van's frame rail served as a significant piece of evidence in catching those responsible for the crime.

the NYPD bomb squad—got close enough to the blast seat to finally examine the rubble itself. Their flashlight beams played across piles of almost indistinguishable fragments. Suddenly, ATF bomb expert Joseph Hanlin said, "Hey, look at this."

Hanlin picked up an 18-inch twisted hunk of yellow metal. His practiced eye recognized the soot-covered fragment as a piece of the frame rail from a van or truck. Its strangely contorted shape led him to conclude that it had been extremely close to the blast. When he turned it over, he could read five scorched but decipherable numbers: part of a long string of numerals known as a vehicle identification number (VIN). VINs are stamped on various parts of every motor vehicle when it is manufactured; the numerical codes for a vehicle's make, model, and year are used by police to help trace or identify it if it is stolen or wrecked.

Hanlin passed the piece of metal to his colleagues to examine. "There were ten million pieces down there," said Lt. Walter Moser, commander of the New York Police Department bomb squad, "but this [one] struck everyone." After investigators cleaned the piece, they could clearly read the VIN: the vehicle was manufactured by Ford Motor Company. Ford checked its records and discovered that the VIN matched that of a yellow Ford Econoline E-350 van that had been sold to the Ryder Truck Rental Company in Alabama. Ryder officials in Alabama identified the license plate as XA-70668, recently rented out of the company's Jersey City office.

On the morning of Wednesday, March 3, three days after investigators found the van fragment, the FBI phoned the Jersey City Ryder office and told franchise owner Patrick Galasso it needed to speak to him.

"He Didn't Have a Clue"

Patrick Galasso told the FBI that he had no trouble remembering who rented the van with license plate number XA-70668. It was Mohammed Salameh, who had come to the office for the second time two days earlier, insisting that the van had been stolen and demanding that the company return his $400 deposit. A Ryder representative had told Salameh once more that he could not repay the deposit until the man filed a police report. Salameh left but vowed to come on Wednesday for his money—the day the FBI spoke with Galasso.

Ramzi Yousef and Eyyad Ismoil were already out of the country and Mahmud Abouhalima had arranged to flee to Sudan on Tuesday. Left behind in the United States, Salameh and Nidal Ayyad were becoming desperate to escape. That Monday, the day he had stormed out of the Ryder office,

Salameh purchased a plane ticket for a Friday flight to Amsterdam, the Netherlands. He believed that would give him a few more days to recover his rental deposit. As for Ayyad, he would have to fend for himself.

Outside the World Trade Center on Monday, February 29, a strange scene unfolded. Office workers in suits and tailored overcoats gratefully accepted steaming cups of coffee from Red Cross workers. Having arrived at the usual time to begin the workday, employees of 900 companies housed in the building learned that the towers were inaccessible. Only small groups at a time were permitted into the complex for 30-minute intervals to collect whatever essential equipment or records they needed. Then they had to leave. Employees were given instructions and an index card printed with a number indicating which group they were assigned to. Thousands of people held cards and waited. Fears over the explosion had abated, but many were still on edge. "Boredom is a great remedy for fear," commented Ted Beck, an officer with Sumitomo Bank Capital Markets Inc., who was among the workers lined up outside.

Some companies couldn't afford to wait. Gao Gui Ming, the CEO of a tiny import-export firm called Shantra New York, retreated to his apartment in Battery Square Park to work. "All you really need is a phone line, a desk, a computer, and a fax machine," Ming told a reporter optimistically. Okisan International America, a 10-person operation, became a one-man business when its president set up shop in a friend's office on Park Avenue. That weekend, the New York-based telephone company NYNEX handled 7,000 requests to reroute business calls from World Trade Center lines to different phone numbers.

Most workers from the World Trade Center towers had no choice but to wait outside, however. The law firm of Tacher, Proffitt & Wood lost between $150,000 and $200,000 in billings in one day. A half-dozen New York

Shipping Association workers paced back and forth. Unless they could retrieve 30 boxes of pension checks, 14,400 retired longshoremen wouldn't be paid. Eric Brown of Arjay Telecom, Inc. tried to make the best of the situation through some charitable advertising—he gave firefighters, police, and others free batteries for their communication devices. At Lynn's Hallmark Card Shop in the World Trade Center concourse, manager John Torres said, "I hope this ends soon. I've got $35,000 worth of chocolate bunnies coming in for Easter that I've got to sell."

One of the few people allowed to work inside the building was complex director Charles Maikish. On his desk, he found the lease he had been signing at the moment of the explosion, with flecks of soot spotting the top page. He brushed them off and saw that he had written only the first letter of his last name before dropping the pen. He realized then that signing a lease was such a simple responsibility, compared to the work that lay ahead.

First, the damaged basement levels had to be cleared of rubble. In two 10-hour shifts, about 240 workers pulled debris from the pit using a crane. The scrap was pulled up through a 30-foot hole specially dug in the Trade Center plaza for the operation. Eugene Fasullo, the Port Authority's chief engineer, explained to reporters that removing shattered pieces of the building from level B-6 was like playing a game of pick-up sticks. "If you pick up the wrong stick, the whole thing collapses," he warned. Over three weeks, two welders on a catwalk suspended in the crater used 180 40-foot steel tubes to provide horizontal and diagonal bracing for the damaged columns.

Restoring electricity to the building was essential. Even the subway tracks beneath the building had no power. Maikish pressured electricians to repair the major electrical switches quickly. The repairmen bridged thousands of feet of severed wiring in the fire-alarm system to restore the building's adherence to safety codes. In just one week, 20 electricians cleaned and tested 3,000 smoke detectors—a job that normally takes six months.

Outside in the cold February air, glaziers rushed to replace hundreds of shattered windows, including several four-story panes in the lobby of WTC 2. From the basement, pumps drew 2 million gallons of water from the basement and plumbers recharged 1.4 million feet of sprinkler-system pipe. Rented refrigeration units on trucks provided air circulation throughout the complex. All vital services were back on-line within two weeks. Then 2,700 workers were sent in to clean the towers and restore them to their pre-blast condition. In 10 days, they had completed both towers.

Six weeks after the World Trade Center bombing, all tower offices were fully ready to be occupied once more. For many businesses, however, it was too late. Displaced for weeks and unable to respond to customers quickly, 150 businesses failed—financial casualties of the World Trade Center bombing.

On Tuesday, March 2, four days after the explosion, Mahmud Abouhalima flew from New York to Sudan via Saudi Arabia on a one-way ticket, without family or luggage. The following day, the FBI spoke with Patrick Galasso, owner of the Ryder rental office. In the hope that Mohammed Salameh would carry out his promise to return for his deposit that day, FBI agents staked out the rental office and waited. The hours ticked by, but Salameh didn't show.

At 6 P.M., editors from New York City's *Newsday* called the city's FBI unit. They knew about the Ryder office connection to the bombing, and as a courtesy they were informing the investigators that they were running the story about the van in the Thursday morning edition.

James Fox, head of the New York City FBI unit, decided against asking *Newsday* to wait. He realized that other newspapers and radio stations most likely had similar information. His best hope was that the $400 deposit was important enough to Salameh that he would return to the Ryder office on Thursday.

Fox then recruited Patrick Galasso to entice Salameh by offering to refund his deposit. Galasso did so by phone Thursday morning, and when Salameh agreed to come in, the FBI stakeout resumed. Disguised as Ryder employees, members of the FBI and NYPD joint task force took up positions behind the office counter, along with Galasso and manager Connie Bello.

To their shock, two TV news trucks pulled up outside.

Investigators traced the information from the debris of the Ryder truck to this rental office in Jersey City, New Jersey. Undercover FBI agents apprehended Mohammed Salameh when he returned to reclaim the deposit for the truck that he alleged was stolen.

They had seen the *Newsday* story that morning. Bello ran outside. "You've got the wrong Ryder agency," she lied. They drove away. Next, two Jersey City police officers walked in unexpectedly, announcing that they were checking out the report by a man named Mohammed Salameh that his van had been stolen. Galasso warned them to get out of sight.

At 10:15 A.M., Salameh entered the office.

"Hey, Mohammed, what's happening?" Galasso said. He pointed to the FBI agent beside him. "This is a Ryder rep to help you with your claim." Salameh repeated his story about the van being stolen. No, he said, he didn't have a police stolen vehicle report. The FBI agent listened, then told Salameh that he could only get back $200. Salameh loudly demanded more. Take it or leave it, the agent insisted. Salameh finally took the money and stalked out of the office toward a bus stop. Just as he was about to board, he was surrounded by eight FBI agents. One clapped a pair of handcuffs on his wrists, while another searched him for weapons.

Still in the terrorist's pocket was a copy of the rental agreement, all the blanks for addresses and phone numbers filled in properly, with smears of bomb residue on the paper. Said an astonished FBI source, "I hate to say he masterminded this. I would use the word 'no-mind.'" Galasso expressed his amazement as well. Mohammed Salameh "didn't have a clue. He just wanted the money." Even more blunt was a New York City detective who had been one of the first to peer into the bomb crater. "I cannot believe," he said, "that such devastation could be caused by someone so dumb."

At the White House that afternoon, George Stephanopoulos, President Clinton's communications director, called a press conference to confirm that an arrest had been made in the World Trade Center bombing.

With Salameh in custody, the investigation gathered speed. On the rental agreement, Salameh had written his correct phone number. Agents traced the number to his apartment, where they found Abdul Yasin, the brother of Musab, a member of the wider circle of conspirators that had welcomed Ramzi Yousef the previous fall. While agents rummaged through Salameh's belongings—uncovering wiring, electromagnetic devices and other bomb-related tools—bomb-sniffing dogs reacted to something in a closet. Looking on, Yasin quickly expressed his eagerness to assist the FBI.

With remarkable cool, Yasin volunteered the address of the bomb-making factory at 40 Pamrapo Avenue and offered the investigators all the information they requested. His behavior must have been persuasive. Despite being an Iraqi living in the United States for only six months, Yasin received the FBI's thanks and was released from the Newark headquarters where he was questioned. The next day, Yasin boarded Royal Jordanian Flight 262 to Amman, Jordan—the same plane Salameh had hoped to catch—and then continued to Baghdad.

At the Al-Salam mosque in Jersey City, Abdel-Rahman put on a convincing show as well when FBI agents questioned him. The sheik denounced the bombing and said he had never heard of Mohammed Salameh. In any event, investigators had enough evidence to bring Salameh before Judge Richard Owen for arraignment on Thursday in Manhattan federal district court. Reporters jammed the courtroom as Salameh, handcuffed and wearing sneakers and a baggy gray sweatsuit, was led in by federal marshals. Robert Precht, Salameh's court-appointed attorney, requested an Arabic interpreter for his client. As Judge Owen read the charges against him an FBI translator leaned close to Salameh and repeated them: the suspect had aided and abetted the World Trade Center

In the aftermath of the explosion, many businesses operating in the World Trade Center tower had to relocate; here, an employee carts his company's supplies away from the building.

bombing, had helped kill five people (the body of Wilfredo Mercado had not yet been discovered), and had violated federal antiterrorism statutes, for which the death penalty could be imposed. Salameh pleaded not guilty and requested bail. The judge refused, calling Salameh a "serious risk" and ordering him kept in custody until his hearing on March 18.

Salameh insisted that he was an innocent man being persecuted for his religious beliefs. He requested a copy of the Koran, a wristwatch so that he could worship at proper times, and a change in his meal schedule so he could observe daytime fasting during the Muslim holy month of Ramadan. On March 5, the day after Salameh's arraignment, federal agents discovered a truckload of chemical explosives components at the Space Station storage shed rented in Salameh's name. At the Brooklyn address on Salameh's driver's license, which was different from the one where he had been living, they found a mailbox bearing the names of Ibrahim El-Gabrowney and his cousin, the imprisoned El Sayyid Nosair.

As investigators entered El-Gabrowney's apartment, he rushed into the bathroom and plunged his hands into a urine-filled toilet bowl to foil attempts at testing his hands for traces of explosives. Then he punched two agents who were searching the apartment. Found among his belongings were fraudulent Nicaraguan passports for Nosair and his family, as well as Nosair's valid U.S. passport, a 9-mm pistol, and 150 rounds of ammunition. Judge Owen charged El-Gabrowney later that day with conspiracy in connection with the World Trade Center bombing.

The FBI's next stop was Maplewood, New Jersey, where Nidal Ayyad lived. The chemical engineer's business card had been found in one of Salameh's pockets during a search. Agents arrested Ayyad on Wednesday, March 10. Three days later, Egyptian police made their own arrest in Kafr el-Dawar—they seized Mahmud Abouhalima, the "outside man" for the conspirators, who had fled New York City four days after the bombing.

The Egyptian police, however, were unwilling to release Abouhalima to the United States immediately. Instead, for more than two weeks he was held in secret. His attorney later protested that Egyptian police tortured and beat him. Finally, a family member called Abouhalima's brother in the United States, who informed the FBI that the hunted man was in custody in Egypt. Reluctantly, the police

FBI agents escort terror-
ist Mahmud Abouhalima
through a federal build-
ing. After the February
23 bombing, Abouhalima
fled to Egypt, where he
was apprehended a few
weeks later and handed
over to U.S. authorities.

released him, but they did so under a U.S. arrest warrant to
avoid alerting Muslim radicals that he was being extradited
to stand trial.

Abouhalima arrived at an airport in upstate New
York on March 31, accompanied by three FBI agents and
a New York City police detective who had retrieved him
in Cairo. Armed guards transported the terrorist in a 12-
car motorcade to a New York City prison just a dozen
blocks from the World Trade Center. That same day,
Ramzi Yousef, his whereabouts still unknown, was also
indicted in connection with the bombing.

The swiftness of the arrests convinced Abdel-Rahman
that there was an informant among his followers. He was
right, of course—Emad Salem had been installed in the

jihad office by the FBI during Nosair's trial. Even though they had since cut off contact with Salem, authorities had been able to track the bombers because they left a relatively easy trail. Now, however, believing an informant was still active, the sheik loudly proclaimed his own innocence. As the FBI rounded up the bombing conspirators, Abdel-Rahman publicly denied knowing Mohammed Salameh, El Sayyid Nosair—who was taped discussing weapons training with the sheik—or Mahmud Abouhalima, who had once been Abdel-Rahman's driver.

On Thursday, April 1, in Manhattan's U.S. District Court, the FBI produced five of the six known suspects in the World Trade Center bombing: Mahmud Abouhalima, Mohammed Salameh, Nidal Ayyad, Ibrahim El-Gabrowney, and Bilal Alkaisi, a previously unknown conspirator who had turned himself in that day. All five pleaded not guilty. Ramzi Yousef was still at large.

"I swear on the Koran, my wife, my children and my family and all I hold dear to me that I am not guilty and had nothing to do with this," Nidal Ayyad declared, despite the overwhelming evidence against him. James Esposito, however, the head of the FBI office in Newark, New Jersey, told reporters, "The circle is now very narrow."

"Death to Murderers!"

Federal marshals place Sheik Omar Abdel-Rahman, the spiritual leader of the terrorist group, into a car after bringing him to New York City by helicopter. Although Abdel-Rahman was considered a suspect in the bombings, he was first apprehended on charges of illegal citizenship.

6

As spring turned into summer and the five World Trade Center conspirators in custody awaited trial, Omar Abdel-Rahman became obsessed with two goals. He was determined first to uncover the informant in his circle of followers, and he planned a new wave of terrorist bombings against the United States.

The informant problem was extremely serious. How had the Egyptian police known where to look for Abouhalima? The world of terrorism was a shadowy place of double identities and false addresses; yet the Egyptian police had captured their prey. The sheik recorded on tape his thoughts about the mystery. In his musings he mentioned one name several times— that of Siddiq Ibrahim Siddiq Ali, a Sudanese national who had helped Abouhalima calculate the amount of explosives needed for the bombing.

As it happened, the spy was indeed someone close to him, but it was not Siddiq Ali. Another regular at the *jihad* office in Brooklyn, Abdu Muhammad Hajjaj, had tipped off the Egyptian police as to Abouhalima's whereabouts. It is unclear whether Hajjaj was an agent of the Egyptian government or was acting independently. One thing was certain, however: Abdel-Rahman unknowingly had been foiled by Hajjaj once before. He had interfered in the sheik's plan to assassinate Egyptian president Hosni Mubarak.

Islamic fundamentalists despised Mubarak as a moderate politician who continued the policies of his predecessor, Nobel Peace Prize–winner Anwar Sadat, assassinated by radicals in 1981. When Egypt announced that Mubarak would visit New York City a month after the World Trade Center bombing, the coincidence must have seemed like a great stroke of luck to Abdel-Rahman and his followers. After Abouhalima's arrest, the sheik gave Siddiq Ali a standing order—to kill Mubarak during the Egyptian president's U.S. visit. After Siddiq Ali consulted his friend Hajjaj for assistance, Hajjaj informed the Egyptian government. Abdel-Rahman suspected that Mubarak's sudden change of plans had to do with Siddiq Ali.

Despite his suspicions, however, the sheik put Ali in charge of another job scheduled for June of that year. It was planned as a "day of terror," during which the United Nations complex and the Lincoln and Holland Tunnels would be bombed. Casualties were expected to be high, and following these successes, the terrorists would hit not only the New York headquarters of the FBI, but also several U.S. military installations and a number of political officials, judges, and foreign heads of state.

Following Mubarak's planned visit to the United

Hosni Mubarak waves to his audience after taking the oath of presidency for Egypt. Omar Abdel-Rahman's group had planned to assassinate President Mubarak during his U.S. visit, but an informant in the sheik's organization exposed the conspiracy to the FBI.

States, Abdel-Rahman, flanked by Siddiq Ali, boasted about upcoming acts of terror. Americans, he warned in June, would be made to pay a terrible price for supporting the Egyptian president. Days later, Siddiq Ali and his mostly Sudanese recruits were surprised and arrested by the FBI while manufacturing bombs. The sweep netted eight terrorists, including Abdel-Rahman himself. Eventually, 15 alleged conspirators were tried in connection with the plot. The sheik bid farewell to his followers and urged them to "give a civilized appearance to Islam" by not resisting the law. "[W]e are not conspiring against America, even though we disagree with American policy," he declared blandly.

Waiting outside the mosque where he spoke were

agents from the INS. Months earlier, Abdel-Rahman had applied for political asylum in the United States, the target of his contempt and schemes. His application was still under review when the new bomb plot surfaced. "The Egyptians definitely don't want the guy back, and we don't want to send him back to Sudan [where he had illegally received a U.S. visa]," a State Department official said at the time. "Nobody has thought through what we do with him after we grab him." Congressman Benjamin Gilman, a member of the House Foreign Affairs Committee, examined a report about the sheik's illegal visa, which Abdel-Rahman had been granted after fleeing Egypt. Gilman called the sequence of events an example of "unbelievable bungling" and blasted the "incompetence and indifference" of U.S. embassy officials in Sudan. New York senator Alfonse D'Amato hotly demanded that Abdel-Rahman be imprisoned. Finally, the sheik was taken into custody, following a U.S. immigration law provision that allows the U.S. attorney general to detain any illegal alien who is likely to flee or who is a "danger to the community." Barbara Nelson, Abdel-Rahman's lawyer, protested, claiming that the U.S. government had "caved in to political pressure."

As a result of this process, Omar Abdel-Rahman surrendered quietly to INS agents for being an illegal U.S. resident, rather than to federal agents for his involvement in the bombing conspiracy. Across the street from the mosque and behind police barricades, Hasidic Jews shouted "Go to hell!" and "Death to murderers!" as the INS took the sheik away. State Department spokesman Michael McCurry said that, although he knew of no specific threat from Abdel-Rahman's followers, the United States was asking diplomatic posts abroad to review their security procedures.

Standing before U.S. District Judge Michael B. Mukasey in a heavily guarded courtroom, Abdel-Rahman and his followers, hands manacled behind their backs, stood silently as the charges against them were recited. In addition to being charged for planning the World Trade Center bombing, the defendants were also accused of planning to assassinate Egyptian president Hosni Mubarak and of conspiring to bomb United Nations headquarters and two New York tunnels.

This marked the first time that Abdel-Rahman had been indicted in the United States. Reporters noted that among the indicted was El Sayyid Nosair, who had been imprisoned on weapons charges related to the murder of Rabbi Meir Kahane. Nosair was now charged with "violence by racketeering" in connection with Kahane's death, because federal prosecutors had new evidence of his involvement in the murder. The indictment alleged that the killing was actually part of the "war of urban terrorism" waged by Abdel-Rahman and others.

All 15 defendants pleaded not guilty and were held without bail. Not long afterward, the U.S. State Department received a declaration signed by three radical groups based in Egypt. "We will take revenge on all U.S. interests and citizens, either in Egypt or outside, if any harm occurs to Sheik Omar [Abdel-Rahman]." As a result, the State Department issued a warning to Americans who were traveling abroad in case the threats were carried out.

In August 1993, six months after the World Trade Center bombing, the trial of the four key conspirators in the disaster began in New York City. (Bilal Alkaisi, who had surrendered to authorities on April 1, was charged with aiding and abetting the bombers; his case would be tried separately.) Ahmad Ajaj, who had been intercepted by immigration authorities when he arrived in the country with Ramzi Yousef in September 1992, was temporarily released from prison to stand trial. Joining him were Mohammed Salameh, the renter of the Ryder truck; Nidal Ayyad, the chemical engineer; and Mahmud Abouhalima, the cab driver extradited from Egypt.

Most Americans who followed the trial expected a great deal of drama as the details of the bombing played out in the courtroom. After all, the defendants had plotted to kill 250,000 people. Only a series of merciful circumstances and the building's ability to withstand a powerful blast had prevented the almost unimaginable destruction the conspirators had planned. In the minds of most people, Salameh, Ayyad, Abouhalima, Ajaj, and the missing Ramzi Yousef were the perpetrators of the worst act of terrorism the United States had ever experienced.

The trial was less than spectacular, however; at times it was remarkably boring. For five months, the jury of eight women and four men shifted in their chairs and listened as the government called 207 witnesses and produced 1,000 models, maps, photographs, and plastic bags of evidence containing pieces of the Ryder van and shards of the hydrogen tanks used in the explosion. Rarely did anything disturb the solemn procedures. The grim atmosphere deepened when, in mid-November, Ahmad Ajaj and Bilal Alkaisi attempted suicide in their cells. Along with several other defendants, the two had been on a hunger strike to protest prison conditions, which included 23 hours of solitary confinement daily and restrictions on group prayer.

In what one journalist called a "masterly six-hour summation" at the conclusion of the trial, U.S. attorney Henry DePippo "wove together phone calls, finger-prints, chemical analysis, chunks of metal, and parking stubs into a narrative that led to the on-ramp of the B-2

Three New York City police officers stand guard as an Islamic man enters the U.S. District Court in New York City. During the trials of the bombers that began in January 1995, officials tightened the courtroom's security.

parking level of the World Trade Center." DePippo focused on the roles that Mohammad Salameh, Nidal Ayyad, Mahmud Abouhalima, and Ahmad Ajaj had played in the "deadly act."

"Lies and deception," countered Abouhalima's attorney to the accusations. Ayyad's lawyer spoke for four hours; at one point during his speech even the judge fell asleep. Salameh's lawyer startled his fellow defense attorneys—and his client—by arguing that there had indeed been a plot, but that Salameh had been duped by Ramzi Yousef, the operation's mastermind. Salameh was so outraged at being characterized as a stooge that three days later he formally objected to his lawyer's summation in a letter to the judge. "I would never have agreed to [it] had it been told me," he said of the argument. Ajaj's lawyer called for a mistrial, but the judge denied the motion.

Finally, the jury returned a verdict on the 38 charges against the defendants. On conspiracy to bomb buildings: guilty. On explosive destruction of property: guilty. On assault on a federal officer: guilty. They were found guilty on an exhaustive list of charges. As the jury forewoman finished announcing the verdict, the defendants lashed out in rage. "Injustice! We are the victims!" shouted Mohammad Salameh, pointing at the jurors and pounding his fist on the table. "*Allah-Akbar* [God is great]!" and "*Al-Nasr lil-Islam* [Victory to Islam]!" shouted the other defendants. From the gallery, Nidal Ayyad's brother screamed, "You are all . . . liars! My brother is innocent!" The judge sentenced each of the four conspirators to 240 years in prison.

"The message of this verdict is twofold," said FBI deputy assistant director William Gavin after the trial concluded. "That terrorism has invaded the shores of the United States of America, and that you will be caught, prosecuted and may go to jail [for attempting it]."

Following Omar Abdel-Rahman's arrest in the summer of 1993, his supporters mounted a website to raise funds for his defense. One of the attorneys who joined the defense team was the former attorney general of the United States, Ramsey Clark.

The trial of Abdel-Rahman and nine other defendants began on January 9, 1995, in Manhattan. The sheik and his followers faced charges of seditious conspiracy and several other crimes in the June 1993 plot to bomb New York landmarks. Charges of sedition were

also levied for the defendants' involvement in the
World Trade Center bombing, and they were charged
with attempting to assassinate prominent politicians
and foreign leaders. Government prosecutors planned
to argue that the effort to blow up several structures,
including the World Trade Center, was part of a "war of
urban terrorism against the United States." This war,
they intended to prove, was directed by Omar Abdel-
Rahman against people the defendants viewed as infidels
and enemies of Islam. "They don't have a case," said one
Abdel-Rahman follower confidently. In fact, up to that
point, Abdel-Rahman had never been convicted of
anything more serious than falsifying a check—one of
the infractions for which the State Department was
trying to have him deported.

As the trial was called in session, Abdel-Rahman,
wearing his trademark red-and-white Islamic cap, dark
glasses, and light blue prison clothing, kept his head
lowered and listened to an Arabic translation through
headphones. "The struggle begins," the sheik was heard
to say by one of his attorneys, Harry Batchelder.

Law enforcement officials were understandably con-
cerned over the possibility of terrorist acts during the
trial itself. More than 40 federal marshals circled the
crowded courtroom. Outside, dozens of New York
policemen patrolled the courthouse corridors, steps, and
sidewalks. Two bomb-sniffing dogs constantly moved
through the building.

During the early days of the trial, government
prosecutors made clear that they would rely heavily
on statements made by Abdel-Rahman himself, many
of which had been secretly recorded by Emad Salem,
the FBI's one-time informant. They planned to prove
to the jury that the sheik's speeches, recorded threats,
and even his sermons were proof that he instructed his

followers to commit acts of terrorism. Abdel-Rahman's attorneys responded swiftly and moved to dismiss all charges. The accusations against their client, they argued, added up to "no evidence of criminal conduct . . . even with government innuendo and unsupportable characterizations of tape recorded statements."

Although the motion was denied, the defense attorneys had revealed the essence of their strategy: that remarks, no matter how angry or inflammatory, are not crimes. The sheik was no ringleader, they said. His statements were mere expressions of opinion and were protected by the First Amendment to the U.S. Constitution. Abdel-Rahman's attorneys asserted that he was on trial merely for expressing views that the government did not like and that there was no proof linking him to criminal activity. Therefore, they argued, he could not have led the other defendants to commit acts of terrorism.

The prosecution methodically cited speeches Abdel-Rahman had made in Detroit and in other U.S. cities, in which he urged his followers to "conquer the land of the infidels to purify it." They pointed out that, although an Egyptian court had cleared Abdel-Rahman personally of participation in Anwar Sadat's assassination, he himself later claimed credit for it. They played tape-recorded conversations in which the defendant boasted that the Islamic Group to which he belonged in Egypt had "carried out many *jihad* operations. . . . The most famous and the most successful operation was fighting the atheist, the oppressor and the profligate by killing him— Anwar al-Sadat, that is; and now, it is hoping for another operation, God willing."

This other "operation," the prosecution argued, was a planned assassination of Sadat's successor, Hosni Mubarak. Tapes proved that the sheik described his authority to issue *fatwas* (Islamic orders) against the likes of Sadat and Meir Kahane as an "honor and something to be proud of." And in one of the most powerful passages introduced by the prosecution, Omar Abdel-Rahman clearly identified himself as a terrorist:

> Why do we fear the word terrorist? If the terrorist is the person who defends his right, so we are terrorists. And if the terrorist is the one who struggles for the sake of Allah, then we are terrorists. We . . . have been ordered with terrorism because we must prepare what power we can to terrorize the enemy of Allah. The Koran [calls on us] "to strike terror," therefore we don't fear to be described as "terrorists." . . . Let them say what they wish to say. . . . We are ordered to prepare whatever we can of power to terrorize the enemies of Islam.

The trial lasted nine months. On October 1, 1995, the jury found Abdel-Rahman and the nine other defendants guilty on 48 of 50 charges, including seditious conspiracy, solicitation and conspiracy to murder Hosni Mubarak, solicitation to attack a U.S. military installation, and conspiracy to conduct bombings. In the only acquittals, Ibrahim El-Gabrowney and El Sayyid Nosair were found not guilty of the June 1993 plot to bomb New York City landmarks. However, they were found guilty of the broader conspiracy charge. Nosair, already in prison on a lesser charge connected to the murder of Meir Kahane, was now convicted of committing the murder.

Amid intense security in and around the courthouse, Judge Mukasey handed down stiff sentences. After Abdel-Rahman received life in prison without parole, he delivered a long, impassioned speech in Arabic. "This case is nothing but an extension of the American war against Islam," he declared through an interpreter. Among the other defendants, the harshest sentence was imposed on Nosair, who received life in

These two photographs, taken from an FBI video that prosecutors showed during the trial of the terrorists, dramatize what happened before and after the bomb inside the Ryder van exploded in the World Trade Center.

prison. His cousin, El-Gabrowney, received 57 years for conspiracy and other charges, including possession of false passports and visas. The other seven defendants—Clement Hampton-El, Victor Alvarez, Tarig Elhassan, Mohammed Saleh, Fadil Abdelgani, his cousin Amir Abdelgani, and Fares Khallafalla—received sentences ranging from 25 to 35 years in prison for planning terrorism aimed at changing U.S. policy in the Middle East. "You agreed to participate in a conspiracy to commit a monstrous crime," Judge Mukasey admonished one defendant. Victor Alvarez was portrayed during the nine-month trial as a borderline mentally handicapped man from a broken family; he denied any part in the conspiracy, but the

judge was unmoved. "Forgive me if it sounds cold-hearted," Mukasey said, "but people who are killed by people with limited capacity are just as dead as people killed by geniuses."

Before their individual sentencings, all 10 defendants maintained their innocence. "I am not a terrorist. I condemn terrorism in the world," declared Mohammed Saleh, accused of agreeing to provide fuel oil for the bomb conspiracy. "I ask God Almighty that one day . . . the truth will come out." Clement Hampton-El vowed revenge on the prosecutors in court. "You'll be next," he said to them. "You knew when you brought me here that I was innocent. The day will come for you."

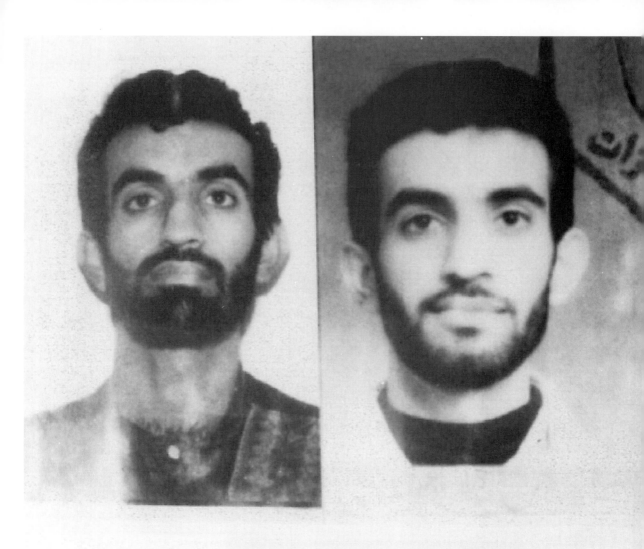

RAMZI AHMED YOUSEF

Date of Birth	May 20, 1967
Place of Birth	Iraq
Race	White
Sex	Male
Eyes	Brown
Hair	Brown
Height	6'0"
Weight	180 pounds
INS A#	A72-054-519

The FBI issued these photographs and description of terrorist leader Ramzi Yousef to the public in an effort to quickly apprehend him. Eventually caught and sentenced to life imprisonment in 1997, Yousef would remain defiant, declaring, "Yes, I am a terrorist, and proud of it."

"Yes, I Am a Terrorist"

After Ramzi Yousef stranded Mohammad Salameh at New York's John F. Kennedy airport, he himself escaped cleanly. With the exception of Eyyad Ismoil, the driver of the van who fled the same night as Yousef, all of the other key players in the World Trade Center bombing stood trial and were imprisoned.

After the bombing, Yousef stayed out of sight for a long while. However, as time passed, and with attention focused on the two New York City bombing trials, Yousef may have believed he could begin to operate more aggressively. On December 11, 1994, still at large after nearly two years and despite the State Department's $2-million bounty on him, Ramzi Yousef resurfaced in the Philippines and tested a new explosive.

This bomb was made of a liquid substance designed to pass unnoticed through airport metal detectors. With the device tucked into a piece of carry-on luggage, Yousef boarded Philippine Air Lines Flight 434 in Manila under the name Armaldo Forlani. He sat in seat 26 and slipped beneath it the package containing the bomb. When the plane landed in Cebu, Yousef deplaned and left the package behind. An explosion rocked the aircraft two hours later, en route to Tokyo, Japan, killing a Japanese businessman who had taken seat 26. The smoke-filled Boeing 747 was forced to land in Okinawa instead.

The bomb had worked perfectly, and now Yousef and the terrorist group he had joined in the Philippines could proceed with their plan. In a 48-hour period in January 1995, they aimed to blow up 11 U.S. airliners in a spectacular display of rage against the United States. A second attack was an anti-Christian assault: they would assassinate Pope John Paul II during his visit to Manila, around the time of their attack on the airlines.

Yousef established headquarters at the Dona Josefa apartment complex in Manila. With the help of his girlfriend, Carol Santiago, and conspirators, Abdel Hakim Murad and Wali Khan, he drew up a map of the Pope's route and collected some Bibles and priest-like robes. The four purchased timing devices, sulfuric acid, and other chemicals for assembling high explosives. But on January 7, five days before the Pope's visit to the Philippines, Yousef started a fire in his apartment while mixing the bomb ingredients. The three men escaped into the street, but when Yousef realized they left behind a laptop computer spelling out their plans, he ordered Murad to retrieve it.

No sooner had Murad reached the apartment than

the Philippine police stormed in and arrested him. Yousef and Santiago eluded capture, probably by fleeing through Muslim territory in the south and then crossing into neighboring Malaysia. Wali Khan was arrested a few days after the fire. Investigators who decrypted Yousef's computer files uncovered the details of the plot, code-named "BOJINKA." Flight schedules and a letter supplied details of the intended bombing of 11 flights to the United States, all on the same day. Four of the participants were to return to Karachi, Pakistan, after the attack; the fifth was to head for Doha, Qatar. Another letter in the computer demanded that Filipino authorities release another terrorist in custody. Unless he was freed, the letter said, they would

Before officials caught up him with him in Pakistan, Ramzi Yousef had joined a terrorist group located in Manila, Philippines. Some of its members were brought to court on charges of carrying explosives.

"make and use chemicals and poisonous gas . . . for use against vital institutions and residential populations and the sources of drinking water" in the Philippines.

U.S. intelligence agents, informed that Yousef's fingerprints had been identified in Manila, alerted law enforcement officials throughout the Pacific region and issued a warning of possible bomb attacks against U.S. airlines traveling in Asia. Still, no one had discovered Ramzi Yousef's whereabouts. One news report speculated that he was part of an unsuccessful plot against the Israeli embassy in Bangkok, Thailand. Another said he had planned to blow up a plane flying out of Thailand. Law enforcement officials pursued Yousef to Bangkok but lost his trail after that. From there, Yousef made his way to Islamabad, Pakistan. He intended to continue to Peshawar, across the Pakistan-Afghanistan border from where he had received his terrorist training.

On February 7, at the two-story Su Casa boarding house in Islamabad, Ramzi Yousef paid for a night in Room 16. The staff said he was polite, but quiet. A porter offered to help him with his two suitcases, but Yousef refused the help.

His arrival did not go unnoticed. At the U.S. embassy, a Muslim approached the regional security officer and informed him that Yousef had just returned from Thailand, "and he's getting ready to leave for Peshawar." He explained that Yousef had hired him to assist in attacks against the United States, but he had seen the State Department's $2-million reward advertised on posters, in videos, and even on matchbook covers. He wanted the money.

At 9:30 the next morning, 10 agents rushed to Su Casa's front desk. "Where's Room 16?" one demanded. A hotel clerk pointed the way and the men ran upstairs.

جريمة بحق الإنسانية.

HELP US FIND THE MISSING TERRORIST, BEFORE HE FINDS MORE INNOCENT VICTIMS.

$2,000,000 REWARD

RAMZI AHMED YOUSEF

"It was like a hurricane, a big panic," said a Pakistani businessman staying in a room on the ground floor. Moments later, the agents hustled Yousef down the stairs, bound at the wrists and legs, blindfolded, and barefoot. "I'm innocent! Why are you taking me?" he shouted. "Show me the arrest warrant!" In his room, investigators found bomb-making equipment that included two toy cars packed with explosives. They also discovered schedules for United and Delta Airlines flights.

James Fox, the former director of the FBI's New York office, pumped his fist in the air upon hearing of Ramzi Yousef's arrest. "Yes! At last!" he cried. Yousef was "the key man" in the World Trade Center bombing,

To track down Ramzi Yousef and his fellow conspirators, the FBI unveiled an aggressive publicity campaign and announced a $2-million reward (right) to anyone who would come forward with information on the fugitive's whereabouts.

he told reporters. "I doubt there would have been an explosion without him." At a press conference, President Clinton hailed the arrest as a "major step forward in the fight against terrorism. Terrorism will not pay. Terrorists *will* pay," he proclaimed.

The man who had launched a two-year worldwide search was placed aboard a military jet and taken to New York. Astonishingly, he chatted with agents on the journey, explaining that he had considered a poison-gas attack on the World Trade Center but that it would have been too costly. "He regretted not killing enough people," assistant U.S. attorney David Kelley marveled. Yousef was arraigned on charges relating to the World Trade Center bombing of February 26, 1993. On April 12, 1995, he was also indicted for conspiring to bomb Philippine Airlines Flight 434 and several other air carriers traveling in the Far East.

Yousef's compatriots in the Middle East watched the arrest and capture and vowed to avenge it. In mid-March, in retaliation for Yousef's extradition to the United States, gunmen killed two U.S. consular officials in Karachi, Pakistan. In August of that year, Eyyad Ismoil, the driver of the Ryder van in the World Trade Center bombing, was also arrested in Jordan and extradited to the United States. Ismoil "smirked" when the aircraft in which he was flying soared above the twin towers of the World Trade Center. He pleaded not guilty to both the bombing and conspiracy.

New Yorkers were understandably uneasy at having international terrorists returned to the scene of their crimes and awaiting trial. A few days after Ismoil was extradited, hundreds of people were evacuated from the World Trade Center when a suspicious package was reported. It turned out to be a broken musical greeting card.

The trial of Ramzi Yousef and his conspirators Abdel Hakim Murad and Wali Khan began on May 13, 1996. Because the FBI had solid evidence, such as the laptop files detailing the plots and Murad's attempt to retrieve it from the chemical fire, the trial was fairly straightforward. The jurors delivered a verdict on September 5: all defendants were guilty. Khan and Murad received life sentences. Yousef's sentencing was suspended until he and Eyyad Ismoil were tried on charges relating to the World Trade Center bombing, in late summer 1997.

During the year that passed between trials, government and defense attorneys prepared for what appeared to be the final chapter in one of the most wildly ambitious terrorist acts in United States history. Four of the conspirators—Mohammad Salameh, Nidal Ayyad, Mahmud Abouhalima, and Ahmad Ajaj—were already behind bars. A larger group of would-be terrorists led by Omar Abdel-Rahman had been tried and convicted as well. Now the prosecution had to reacquaint a jury with the events that led to 12:18 P.M. on February 26, 1993, the moment when the 1,500-pound bomb exploded in the World Trade Center.

At 10:45 P.M. on July 30, just days before the trial was scheduled to begin, a frantic man ran into the middle of a Brooklyn street and flagged down two police officers. "Bomba! Bomba!" he shouted in broken English. Abdel Rahman Mussaba, an Egyptian newly arrived in the United States, said that the men with whom he shared an apartment were planning to blow up the city's subway system. At a police station, an interpreter helped Mussaba describe the men, the layout of the apartment, and the type of bombs they had.

Six hours later, in the pre-dawn of July 31, a police Special Weapons and Tactics (SWAT) team stormed

An armored police car stands parked by the U.S. consulate in Karachi, Pakistan. At this federal building and others in Arab countries, officials stood guard against any terrorist attacks that might result in retaliation for Ramzi Yousef's sentencing on January 8, 1998.

the apartment and ordered two men inside not to move. When one made a grab for an officer's weapon and the other reached toward a black bag, the officers shot and seriously wounded both of them.

The would-be bombers were Gazi Ibrahim Abu Mezer and Lafi Khalil, Palestinians from the West Bank of Israel who, according to that country's television news reports, had "security records." In the apartment, the police recovered a bomb constructed out of four pipes, which were packed with black gunpowder and wired to a single power source. Because the device had no timer (and therefore could not be detonated remotely), police determined that it was a "suicide bomb," meant to kill not only the person who detonated it but also anyone else within 25 feet of the blast. "That thing was all set and ready to go. It is not the kind of thing you plan to keep around unless you plan to use it right away," said New York police commissioner Howard Safir.

A note found in the apartment written in Arabic by Mezer expressed hatred for Jews and Americans, denounced the persecution of Arabs, and bid farewell to his family. A second note, which the two apparently planned to leave behind in a bomb-proof container, called for the release of Ramzi Yousef and Eyyad Ismoil, who were awaiting trial, as well as that of Omar Abdel-Rahman, who was already serving a life sentence. Later, police also found a second bomb, this one wrapped in nails.

News of Abdel Rahman Mussaba's role in averting another terrorist bombing in New York City caused jubilation in his hometown, a tiny village 350 miles south of Cairo, Egypt. Mussaba was an instant hero, and his proud father became the most admired man in town. "The Americans are very happy about what he did," Mussa's brother happily told ABC News. "He saved many lives, children and women and old men." Beaming, his father continued, "He saw what was going on. He was in total shock. . . . He went to the police station." The FBI awarded Mussaba an undisclosed sum of money as a reward for helping to prevent a terrorist act.

Ramzi Yousef and Eyyad Ismoil went on trial before U.S. District Judge Kevin Duffy on August 4, 1996. For the next two months, prosecutors offered the testimonies of more than 100 witnesses. They presented chemical evidence, reports of residue and fingerprints found at bomb-making sites in New Jersey, statements from explosives experts, telephone receipts, and other evidence of the plot. They charged that Yousef and his conspirators mixed chemicals to produce explosives in a Jersey City apartment, and that Yousef conferred with Ismoil by phone before Ismoil traveled to New York to be the driver of the Ryder van.

Sitting in the courtroom was Ismoil's mother, who had flown from Jordan, the first relative of a defendant to attend any of the bombing trials. She spoke to reporters during a break in the trial, saying through an interpreter that she would have preferred her son be tried alone and not with Yousef. "She is so sure Eyyad has nothing to do with this and that is why she would like him to be tried alone," the interpreter said. "[She's] not just saying this as his mother, but he loves America."

Prosecutors portrayed Ramzi Yousef as one of the most sinister terrorists in history and Eyyad Ismoil as his willing accomplice. Over and over, they reminded the jury that Yousef had hoped to topple the World Trade Center's twin towers like giant dominoes, killing as many as 250,000 people. The motive, government lawyers said, was to punish the United States for its support of Israel. Assistant U.S. attorney Lev Dassin explained:

> These defendants bombed the World Trade Center because of their own prejudice and their own hatred for Israel. The defendants thought they were above the law. . . . Yousef knew he wasn't an immigrant seeking a better life. Yousef knew exactly what was going on. He came here to do one thing: to bomb his target.

An especially emotional point in the trial occurred on the day when jurists examined photographs of the bomb victims. Louis Aidala, Ismoil's attorney, tried unsuccessfully to bar prosecutors from presenting graphic details about the victims' deaths. He argued that the photos would inflame and prejudice the jury. Judge Duffy ruled otherwise, declaring that the photos had been used in the earlier trial and were therefore acceptable in this one. Some jurors wept and shuddered at the sight of the disfigured corpses and at the medical examiner's testimony about their violent deaths. The victims died of blunt impact trauma, the medical examiner explained. Yousef stared straight ahead and Ismoil kept his head down as the photographs circulated.

Perhaps most important, prosecutors told the jury, was the fact that even while being extradited to the United States, Ramzi Yousef had expressed his wish that he could have killed more people. Yousef's attorney, Roy Kulcsar, countered that no one had recorded Yousef's statement, and that admitting the crime would only have made his situation worse. "It doesn't make sense how Ramzi Yousef was in the United States with no money and no contacts and somehow becomes the mastermind of the World Trade Center bombing," Kulcsar argued. Ismoil's attorney, Louis Aidala, said his client's role in the bombing was being exaggerated and that anti-Arab bias poisoned the case. Aidala said Ismoil was tricked into helping others carry out the bombing by loading into the van boxes that he thought contained soap and shampoo. Yousef had told him he was setting up a shop in the World Trade Center.

On November 6, 1997, the jury began deliberations. Judge Kevin Duffy's instructions on law concerning the case lasted for more than three hours. The jury returned a verdict in three days: Ramzi Yousef was guilty of masterminding the 1993 bombing of the World Trade Center; Eyyad Ismoil was guilty on charges of driving an explosives-laden van into the basement garage of the complex.

In January 1998 Judge Duffy sentenced Ramzi Yousef to 240 years in federal prison, a sentence that excludes any possibility of parole. At the time of the sentencing, the world got a final glimpse into the mind of the man who

Jajlah Ismoil, mother of Eyad Ismoil, insists on her son's innocence during his trial, which began in August 1997. Ismoil, who drove the Ryder van used in the World Trade Center bombing, was sentenced in April 1998 to 240 years in prison, with no chance of parole, and fined $10 million in restitution.

had traveled the globe in his efforts to kill as many people as he could. Yousef boasted to reporters of his exploits in death. "Yes, I am a terrorist," he declared, "and proud of it."

The World Trade Center bombing of February 26, 1993, destroyed the hope that the United States was immune from terrorist attacks on its own soil. The clumsiness of the bombers and their conspirators in other planned attacks highlighted how easily the terrorists could target the United States. In a 1998 report to Congress, Dale Watson, chief of the FBI's International Terrorism Section, described the challenges facing law enforcement officials fighting terrorist acts.

First, said Watson, "loosely affiliated groups of

like-minded extremists . . . pose a real and significant threat to our security." Many terrorist groups consist of people of various nationalities who are not sponsored by a specific country or organization. These groups "operate on their own terms," so their members can assemble, attack, and disperse quickly. In the case of the World Trade Center bombing, for example, Watson pointed out that most of the bombers had the means to escape the United States and travel across the globe within hours of the blast.

Second, terrorists are making use of advanced technology to further their aims. The bomb built by Ramzi Yousef that exploded on the Japan flight had passed through airport scanners undetected. Several organizations, said Watson, even promote their goals on the Internet, posting pages that include propaganda material and recruiting information.

The third challenge, Watson said, is a battle against what he called the "web of terrorism"—one act of violence leading to another. A year after Omar Abdel-Rahman was sentenced, Islamic fundamentalist gunmen in Egypt killed several foreign tourists visiting Luxor, probably in revenge for Abdel-Rahman's imprisonment. International terrorist Osama bin Laden continues to incite Muslims around the world to mount similar attacks. In an interview with *Newsweek* magazine at his desert camp in Afghanistan in 1999, bin Laden confirmed that civilian Americans are as much a target as U.S. military or government agencies. "Muslim scholars have issued a *fatwa* against any American who pays taxes to his government," he said. "[Such an American] is our target, because he is helping the American war machine against the Muslim nation."

In his congressional report, Watson also said that the

United States government already practices five ways of fighting terrorism: through diplomacy, sanctions against governments, secret operations, military options, and law enforcement. In addition, in 1996 the FBI set up its Counterterrorism Center, made up of representatives from 18 federal agencies including the Central Intelligence Agency, the Defense Intelligence Agency, and the United States Secret Service. The Counterterrorism Center was established with three aims in mind: combating international terrorism, combating domestic terrorism, and employing countermeasures to identify terrorist threats. Along with establishing the center, the FBI has also expanded its number of international offices, especially in locations where threats of terrorist plans are most serious.

Lawmakers have also contributed to a solution with the Antiterrorism and Effective Death Penalty Act (AEDPA) passed in 1996. In addition to enforcing heavier penalties on convicted terrorists, an important provision of the act also obstructs the funding of terrorist groups. The government now works to advise U.S. financial institutions against providing for agencies that meet certain undesired criteria.

Of growing concern to the agencies in the center— and to governments worldwide—is the relatively easy access to chemical, biological, and nuclear materials by terrorist groups. "These weapons of mass destruction represent perhaps the most serious potential threat facing the United States today," Watson reported. As a result, the FBI has devoted additional time and more agents to solving the problem. "We cannot escape the disquieting reality . . . [that] crime and terrorism are carried out on an international scale," Watson said. "The law enforcement response must match the threat. By expanding our first line of defense, we improve the ability of the United States to prevent attacks and respond quickly to those that do occur."

"Given the nature of the evolving terrorist threat and the destructive capabilities now available to terrorists," Dale Watson concluded, "the American people deserve nothing less."

Epilogue

At 8:02 A.M., Eastern Standard Time, on September 11, 2001, American Airlines Flight 11 departed from Boston's Logan Airport in perfect weather, bound for Los Angeles, California.

Minutes later, five men, whom the FBI later identified as Mohammed Atta, Waleed M. Alshehri and Wail Alshehri (possibly brothers), Abdulaziz Alomari, and Satam Al Suqami, hijacked the plane. At 8:28 A.M., air traffic controllers overheard from the cockpit: "Don't do anything foolish. You are not going to get hurt. We have more planes. We have other planes."

Twenty minutes later, at 8:48 A.M., Flight 11 crashed into the upper floors of the North Tower of the World Trade Center, in the lower Manhattan section of New York City. All 92 people aboard were killed. Thousands of office workers had already arrived in both towers. Many people in the crash zone—between the 95th and 103rd floors—died instantly. About 80 chefs, waiters, and kitchen porters were also in the Windows on the World restaurant on the 106th floor of the North Tower. Those on the floors above the 95th had no way to descend, their escape routes cut off by fire.

At 7:58 A.M., Eastern Standard Time, a second passenger aircraft, United Airlines Flight 175, left Boston's Logan Airport, also en route to Los Angeles.

A short time into the flight, hijackers armed with knives, whom the FBI later identified as Marwan Al-Shehhi, Fayez Ahmed, Mohald Alshehri, Hamza Alghamdi, and Ahmed Alghamdi, attacked the crew. Passenger Peter Hanson called his parents and told them that hijackers had taken over the plane and stabbed one of the cabin crew. An unnamed female flight attendant called an emergency number and said that her fellow crew members had been stabbed.

At 9:03 A.M., Flight 175 crashed into the South Tower of the World Trade Center at about the 80th floor, creating a fireball that exploded from the side of the building. All 65 people on board the plane were killed. Many people in the South Tower had witnessed the first crash into

Epilogue

the North Tower and had begun to evacuate; however, they were told to return to their desks, that there was no danger. After the impact, some people in the South Tower jumped to their deaths from the windows rather than waiting to die in the fire.

On the street below, hundreds of firefighters and police arrived at the scene to help the office workers escape. The towers had been built to withstand the impact of a large plane, and it was hoped that the steel cores of both buildings, sheathed in protective concrete, would remain intact for one or two hours, allowing rescue workers enough time to reach people in the towers. Unfortunately, both planes had been filled to capacity with 24,000 gallons of jet fuel for their cross-continental flights, and it would be this jet fuel burning at 14720° F that would ultimately melt the steel frames supporting the towers' floors.

At 10:05 A.M., just one hour after the second crash, the South Tower collapsed, the floors flattening on top of one another. Hundreds of rescue workers and people trying to escape were crushed.

Twenty-four minutes later, at 10:29 A.M., the North Tower collapsed as well. As people on the street ran for their lives, dust clouds of pulverized concrete billowed between the buildings of lower Manhattan, turning the day into night.

In addition to this, that morning at Dulles Airport in Washington, D.C., American Airlines Flight 77 had taken off at 8:10 A.M. en route to Los Angeles. It, too, was hijacked, by men that the FBI identified as Khalid Al-Midhar, Majed Moqed, Nawaq Alhamzi, Salem Alhamzi, and Hani Hanjour. Passengers may have been forced into the rear of the plane. On board was TV commentator Barbara Olson, wife of U.S. Solicitor General Theodore Olson, who phoned her husband to alert him of her and her fellow passengers' plight.

The plane approached the nation's capital from the southwest. Just a few miles from the city, it made a 270-degree turn and headed for the Pentagon, the administrative headquarters of the U.S. military. The plane slammed into the building, killing all 64 people on board and

Epilogue

190 Pentagon workers, many of whom burned to death.

Finally, from Newark, New Jersey, that morning, United Airlines Flight 93, originally scheduled to depart for San Francisco at 8:01 A.M., did not leave until 8:42 A.M. Hijackers armed with knives commandeered the flight. The FBI identified them as Ahmed Alhaznawi, Ahmed Alnami, Ziad Jarrahi, and Saeed Alghamdi.

At least four passengers used mobile phones to call relatives and emergency services, at which time they learned about the earlier crashes. One man, Jeremy Glick, told his wife that he and some other passengers had taken a vote and decided to tackle the hijackers. Another passenger, Thomas Burnett, told his wife: "I know we're all going to die . . . There's three of us who are going to do something about it." Investigators said it was likely that there was a struggle in the cockpit. At 10:03 A.M., the plane crashed into the ground at an estimated 450 mph in rural Somerset County, Pennsylvania, southeast of Pittsburgh, killing all 45 people on board. It is believed that a more extensive disaster, possibly another attack on the nation's capital, was averted by the passengers who tried to take back control of the aircraft from the hijackers. The U.S. Senate considered awarding the Congressional Gold Medal, the highest civilian honor in the United States, to all those on board posthumously.

After the collapse of the World Trade Center, more than 5,000 people were officially declared missing or dead, but the figure was later raised to more than 6,500. New York rescue services worked around the clock, aided by firefighters who arrived from other cities. Five survivors were found in the first 24 hours, but relatively few bodies were recovered in the weeks after the catastrophe.

The site where the twin towers of the World Trade Center had formerly stood became known as "ground zero" for the disaster. The president, George W. Bush, declared a war against terrorism, urging Americans to prepare for a long and unconventional struggle, which until September 11, 2001, had been something that American citizens had viewed only from afar.

References consulted:

"America's Day of Terror." *BBC News.* ("The Four Highjacks" and "Trade Center Disaster.") No date. *http://news.bbc.co.uk/hi/english/static/in_depth/americas/2001/day_of_terror/*

Barker, Kim, et al. "Heroes Stand Up Even in the Hour of Their Deaths." *Chicago Tribune* (30 September 2001): 1-18.

Chronology

1990   *November 5:* El Sayyid Nosair assassinates Jewish Defense League leader Meir Kahane

1992   *September 1:* Ahmad Ajaj and Ramzi Yousef attempt to enter the United States using false passports; Ajaj is detained while Yousef stays at the apartment of Musab Yasin; Yasin's brother Abdul arrives shortly thereafter

October: Mohammed Salameh and Ramzi Yousef rent a garage apartment, where they build a bomb

1993   *February 23:* Salameh rents a Ryder van in Jersey City, New Jersey, which will deliver the explosive

February 26: At 12:18 P.M., the bomb explodes in the World Trade Center; Ramzi Yousef flees to Pakistan

February 28: In the bomb crater, investigators find a shattered part with the van's vehicle identification number, allowing investigators to trace the vehicle to the Ryder rental office where Salameh obtained the vehicle

March 4–18: Police arrest Salameh as he tries to reclaim a deposit on the rented van; federal agents seize chemicals in a shed rented by Salameh; police arrest Nidal Ayyad; Sheik Omar Abdel-Rahman denies involvement in the bombing plot

March 24: Mahmud Abouhalima is arrested in Egypt and returned to the United States

March 31: Ramzi Yousef is indicted in the bombing, although his whereabouts are unknown

June 24: Several followers of Abdel-Rahman are arrested on charges of plotting to bomb bridges, tunnels, and other landmarks around New York; 15 fundamentalist Muslims, including Abdel-Rahman, are ultimately indicted in the plot

August: The first World Trade Center bombing trial begins

1994   *March 4:* Salameh, Ayyad, Abouhalima, and Ajaj are convicted on all charges related to the World Trade Center disaster

Chronology

1995   *January:* In the Philippines, Ramzi Yousef, Abdel Hakim Murad, and Wali Khan abandon their plans to blow up U.S. airliners when their apartment catches fire during the mixing of explosive chemicals; the trial begins of Abdel-Rahman and nine other defendants accused of planning to bomb the United Nations building and other New York landmarks;

      February: Ramzi Yousef is arrested in Pakistan after two years as a fugitive

      October 1: Abdel-Rahman and other defendants receive guilty verdicts on 48 of 50 charges; Nosair is also re-tried and convicted of the murder of Meir Kahane

1996   *May 13:* Ramzi Yousef, Abdel Hakim Murad, and Wali Khan are tried for attempting to blow up 11 U.S. airliners.

      September 5: Yousef, Murad, and Khan are found guilty; Yousef's sentencing is suspended until later trial

1997   *July 31:* Pipe bombs targeted for the New York subway system are discovered in a New York City apartment and are traced to two terrorists sympathetic to the Trade Center bombers

      August 4: The second trial involving the World Trade Center bombers begins

      November: Ramzi Yousef and Eyyad Ismoil are found guilty

1998   *January:* Mastermind of the World Trade Center bombing Ramzi Yousef is sentenced to 240 years in prison

      April: Last World Trade Center bombing conspirator, Eyad Ismoil, receives sentence of 240 years and a fine of $10 million

Further Reading

Books

Dwyer, Jim. *Two Seconds Under the World: Terror Comes to America—The Conspiracy Behind the World Trade Center Bombing.* Upland, Mich.: Diane Publishing Co., 1999.

Harmon, Daniel E. *The FBI.* Philadelphia: Chelsea House Publishers, 2001.

Heymann, Philip B. *Terrorism and America.* Cambridge, Mass.: The MIT Press, 1998.

Hoffman, Bruce. *Inside Terrorism.* New York: Columbia University Press, 1999.

Jeffreys, Diarmuid. *The Bureau: Inside the Modern FBI.* Boston: Houghton Mifflin, 1995.

Kerson, Adrian. *Terror in the Towers: Amazing Stories from the World Trade Center Disaster.* New York: Random House, 1993.

Marcovitz, Hal. *Terrorism.* Philadelphia: Chelsea House Publishers, 2001.

Nash, Jay Robert. *Terrorism in the 20th Century.* New York: M. Evans and Co., Inc., 1998.

Schlagheck, Donna M. *International Terrorism.* Lexington, Mass.: Lexington Books, 1988.

Sherrow, Victoria. *The World Trade Center Bombing: Terror in the Towers.* Springfield, N.J.: Enslow Publishers, 1998.

Websites

Federation of American Scientists
"Dale Watson's Statement Before the Senate Judiciary Committee."
http://www.fas.org/irp/congress/1998_hr/s980224w.htm

International Association for Counterterrorism and Security Professionals
http://www.iacsp.org

NY Cop Online Magazine
"World Trade Center Bombing."
*http://www.nycop.com/archives/December_00/WORLD_TRADE_
CENTER_BOMBING/body_world_trade_center_bombing.html*

National Security Institute
"Backgrounder: Terrorism."
http://nsi.org/library/terrorism/facterr.html

World Trade Center
Virtual Tours.
http://www.fieldtrip.com/ny/24357379.htm
http://www.wtc-top.com/

Index

Index

CHARLES J. SHIELDS writes from his home near Chicago, Illinois, where he lives with his wife, Guadalupe, an elementary school principal. Shields was chairman of the English Department at Homewood-Flossmoor High School in Flossmoor, Illinois. This is his third book for Chelsea House Publishers.

JILL McCAFFREY has served for four years as national chairman of the Armed Forces Emergency Services of the American Red Cross. Ms. McCaffrey also serves on the board of directors for Knollwood—the Army Distaff Hall. The former Jill Ann Faulkner, a Massachusetts native, is the wife of Barry R. McCaffrey, formerly a member of President Bill Clinton's cabinet and director of the White House Office of National Drug Control Policy. The McCaffreys are the parents of three grown children: Sean, a major in the U.S. Army; Tara, an intensive care nurse and captain in the National Guard; and Amy, a seventh grade teacher. The McCaffreys also have two grandchildren, Michael and Jack.

Picture Credits